Mark Wigan

SEQUENTIAL IMAGES

adj. forming or following in a
logical order or sequence

n. a representation,
the external form of
a person or thing in art

An AVA Book

Published by AVA Publishing SA

Rue des Fontenailles 16, Case postale, 1000 Lausanne 6, Switzerland

Tel: +41 786 005 109

Email: enquiries@avabooks.ch

Distributed by Thames & Hudson (ex-North America)

181a High Holborn, London WC1V 7QX, United Kingdom

Tel: +44 20 7845 5000 Fax: +44 20 7845 5055

Email: sales@thameshudson.co.uk

www.thamesandhudson.com

Distributed in the USA & Canada by:

Watson-Guptill Publications, 770 Broadway, New York, New York 10003

Fax: +1 646 654 5487

Email: info@watsonguptill.com

www.watsonguptill.com

English Language Support Office

AVA Publishing (UK) Ltd.

Tel: +44 1903 204 455

Email: enquiries@avabooks.co.uk

All reasonable attempts have been made to trace, clear and credit the copyright
holders of the images reproduced in this book. However, if any credits have been
inadvertently omitted, the publisher will endeavour to incorporate amendments in
future editions.

ISBN 2-940373-60-4 and 978-2-940373-60-4

10 9 8 7 6 5 4 3 2 1

Designed at the NEW Studio (TM)

Original text and photography by Mark Wigan and Austin at NEW (TM)

Original book and series concept devised by Natalia Price-Cabrera

Production and separations by AVA Book Production Pte. Ltd., Singapore

Tel: +65 6334 8173 Fax: +65 6259 9830

Email: production@avabooks.com.sg

CONTENTS

INTRODUCTION: I am an art school   **06**

How to get the most out of this book   **10**

Crafting Visual Narratives

The World of Comics

Characters

NARRATIVE STRATEGIES   **12**

Thinking Sequentially   16

Orchestrating a Sequence   18

Crafting Visual Narratives   22

Visual Grammar   36

Storyboards   40

Film Design   50

Art Direction   52

Obliquity

and Anti-narrative   54

PICTORIAL STORYTELLING   **56**

The World of Comics   60

Alternative Comics   64

Key Exemplars   70

Manga   72

Tales from

the Underground   74

ONCE UPON A TIME…   **78**

Publishing   80

Magical Works   84

World of Wonder   88

Golden Years   92

Characters   94

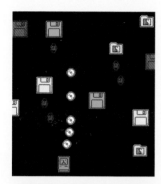

Video Games

Film Noir

Club Visuals

ANIMATION	100
Eclectic Trawl	102
Animation on TV	104
Cult Cartoons	108
Video Games	112

MOVING IMAGE	116
Title Sequences	122
Experimental Film	124
Counterculture	128
Film Theory	132
Genres	134
Film Noir	136
Post-noir	138

AV MASH-UPS	140
Club Visuals	144
Pick 'n' Mix Projects	152
Projects 1, 2, 3, 4	156
Projects 5, 6, 7	157
Projects 8, 9, 10	158
Projects 11, 12, 13, 14	159

Key Term Glossary	160
Graphic Storytelling Charts	162
Reading List and Useful Websites	166
Canon	170
Conclusion	172
Acknowledgements	174
Contacts	175

Description:
Clip artwork and collaborative projects by legendary artist/illustrator/designer Anthony Burrill

I AM AN ART SCHOOL

'Do whatever you do intensely.' Robert Henri, *The Art Spirit*, 1923

Identifying and articulating a personal direction as an illustrator is achieved by taking a critical position on the arts and synthesising processes, skills, techniques, media and ideas.

Through the sustained development of an experimental research and practice-based methodology, illustrators are able to locate themselves within a broader cultural context. The awareness of contemporary trends, debates and historical, theoretical, social, cultural, political and professional contexts is fundamental.

Throughout the book I will attempt to highlight a cross-disciplinary and hybrid approach to illustration and explore its relationship to other specialisms and art forms across a broad cultural spectrum.

Schools of art and design separate subject disciplines and specialisms, niche courses and pathways, reinforcing hierarchical and cultural divisions. Students are often faced by limited views on subjects, anti-intellectualism, vocationalism and an emphasis on employability over creativity. However, many practitioners upon graduation ignore discipline boundaries altogether breaking narrow definitions and parameters.

Illustrators challenging the status quo have always operated in the overlapping area between fine art, commerce and design, and make all areas of creative production their own.

'I call myself an illustrator but I am not an illustrator. Instead I paint storytelling pictures which are quite popular but unfashionable.' Norman Rockwell, *Esquire*, 1962

The illustrator communicates with single or multiple images to clarify ideas, solve problems, interpret, amplify and enrich words and tell stories. Sometimes a single image may visually communicate an idea or emotion without the need to produce a series or sequence. A single image, such as a poster, book jacket or political cartoon communicates on a number of levels. Illustrators employ the fundamental visual grammar of design elements such as scale, colour, composition, contrast, repetition, texture, line, perspective, juxtaposition, visual metaphor and syntax.

SEQUENTIAL IMAGES: INTRODUCTION

The viewer/reader interprets and deciphers the layers of content of the visual message from their own point of view and creates a cultural context and meaning. Constructing meaning engages seeing, reading, intuition, analysis, perception, intellect, cognition, values, emotions, editing, selecting and the search for coherence.

Most illustration assignments require the interpretation, decoration, clarification and intensification of a text, theme, concept or idea provided by someone else. Applied artists are faced by limitations and constraints including briefs, deadlines, reproduction, format, budget, the client and target issues.

Each illustrator decides which brief to answer and which client to work for based on their own personal ethos and values. Many feel pride in their trade, profession or medium of expression and relish the opportunity to respond to a brief. The brief gives their work context and the opportunity to collaborate and provide the client with something more than they expected while making a personal, creative visual statement.

Artists have always operated with restrictions and many of the outstanding works throughout the history of art were commissioned by clients or patrons for specific purposes.

Pictorial storytelling has always been a central theme in world art evident in the many paintings illustrating classical Greek mythology, legends, religious or historical events. Driven by the need for autonomy, some illustrators, especially in the fields of children's books, comics, graphic novels and animation also write and illustrate their own text. Some also self-publish, market and distribute their own work in a wide range of media and contexts.

There are illustrators who author visual stories entirely from their own imagination, communicating memories, points of view or obsessions, making statements with their personal vision. Others will rein in personal expression in order to prioritise concept over form and styling, while creating images that instruct, educate, warn or elucidate a text.

Chapter one

NARRATIVE STRATEGIES – Explores imaginative strategies and methodologies employed to construct and orchestrate visual narratives. In-depth research, observational drawing, interpretation, design and the development of a personal visual language are emphasised. Storyboards, film design and art direction are introduced as is the notion of obliquity and anti-narrative.

Chapter two

PICTORIAL STORYTELLING – Contextualises the world of comics from satirical prints to syndicated newspaper strips, 1960s underground comix to examples of contemporary alternative comics and manga.

Chapter three

ONCE UPON A TIME... – Analyses children's picture books, introducing magical and delightful exemplars from the golden age. 21st-century publishing and character licensing and merchandising contexts are introduced. The author also pays his respects to early influences.

Chapter four

ANIMATION – Examines pictures in motion with an eclectic trawl from the praxinoscope to Pixar. Key highlights show how animation has mirrored the evolution of graphic art and the comic book. As satellite, cable and the Web now offer 24-hour animation, we look back at cult Saturday morning TV shows from the 1950s to the 1980s. There is also a surf through the development of video games from Pong to online virtual worlds.

Chapter five

MOVING IMAGE – Recognises the influential and innovative field of motion graphics and film title design. Experimental and independent film-making and video art are also referenced with examples of theories, genres and a case study in film noir and post-noir.

Chapter six

AV MASH-UPS – Charts the evolution of multimedia events, club visuals and the VJ. Pick 'n' mix sequential projects and exercises, glossary, reading list and canon are provided to encourage the reader to be their own art school.

This book introduces different aspects of sequential image making via dedicated chapters for each topic. Each chapter provides numerous examples of work by leading artists, with interview quotes to explain the reasons behind the choices made.

Key illustration principles are isolated so that the reader can see how they are applied in practice.

Clear navigation

Each chapter has a clear running head to allow readers to quickly locate areas of interest.

Introductions

Special section introductions outline basic concepts that will be discussed.

SEQUENTIAL IMAGES : NARRATIVE STRATEGIES

Description:
Ed Gill aka 'the Koolest Artist' (Art Director) with his spray and bubble machines. Photographed by Ali Peck

Art Direction

Innovative use of art direction and design can also be seen in the films of Fritz Lang in Germany, Cavalcanti in France and Sir Alexander Korda who came from Hungary to London via Paris.

The design of British films was enhanced in the 1920s and 1930s by the arrival in the UK of designers such as Vincent Korda (brother of Alexander), Alfred Junge, Erno Metzener, Oscar Werndorff, Lazar Meerson, André Andrejew and Ferdinand Bellan.

Alfred Junge was responsible for the visual design of films such as *Colonel Blimp*, *A Matter of Life and Death* and *Black Narcissus* for Archers Film Productions. Andre Andrejew's drawings were influenced by the work of Gustave Doré, he art directed in Germany, France and England designing sets for Duvivier's *Golem* and Pabst's *Dreigroschenoper* in 1931.

Many of these art directors were firm believers in the future of film as an art form. Hein Heckroth, who designed sets and costumes for theatre, ballet and film, including Michael Powell's *The Red Shoes*, stated that *'all the machinery and all the money in the world will not help to make a good production if you have nothing to say – no idea'*.

Key figures include Ralph Brinton for the design of Carol Reed's *Odd Man Out*, 1946, Norman Arnold for *Hue and Cry* by Ealing Studios, Wilfred Arnold's backgrounds for Alfred Hitchcock's *Blackmail*, Roy Oxley's designs for Sidney Gilliat's *London Belongs to Me*, Lawrence Paul Williams's work on *Brief Encounter*, and production designer William Cameron Menzies storyboarding for *Gone with the Wind*, 1939.

All these designers were able to visualise and interpret stories creating effective, intelligent and lyrical illustrations to highlight the mood, visual rhythm, lighting, background, costumes and architectural planning of scenes.

John Bryan, the designer for *Oliver Twist* and *Great Expectations*, felt that *'a film consists of a series of two-dimensional illustrations in movement thereby introducing a third dimension. The design, therefore, becomes three-dimensional and in essence largely a planning problem.'* *Art and Design in the British Film*, Edward Carrick, 1948

Quotes

Quotes from featured illustrators and from artists throughout history are included.

Examples

Commercial projects from contemporary artists bring the principles under discussion alive visually.

Additional information

Captions are featured where
necessary, as is client, illustrator
and image information.

Written explanations

Key points are explained
and placed in context.

MOVING IMAGE

116 / 117

*Description:
Black Convoy at the
premiere of the 'Wild'
moving image experiment
at the Wayward for
onedotzero 10*

MOVING IMAGE

**Motion graphics is a synthesis of the skill-sets of graphic
designers, illustrators and animators. It integrates film,
animation, graphics and sound. It spans music videos, short
films, computer games, digital effects, installations, new media,
film title sequences, TV commercials, animated stings, idents,
3D graphics and environmental design.**

It is very much a product of the convergence of media available to
the artist through the development of desktop digital film-making.
This cross-media area blurs definitions and is constantly creating
new hybrid forms and contexts. As in any artistic activity, there are
pioneers who are taking the field forward and there are many pale
imitators creating derivative commercial work following on their
heels. Weak ideas can not be hidden by slick and seductive
digital software effects. Concepts, idea generation, research,
storyboarding, design skills and visual flair remain essential
components in the creation of sequential moving image-making.

The antecedents of motion graphics were the early inventors of
motion pictures and trick cinematography, for example, the Lumière
Brothers, Milies and the experimental films of the avant-garde,
Oskar Fischinger, Man Ray, Buñuel, Hans Richter, Vertov, Léger and
animators such as Len Lye and Norman McLaren.

Motion graphics is a highly challenging experimental and
imaginative field. Techniques used can range from the handcrafted
to sophisticated digital pyrotechnics. Contemporary tools utilised
to integrate time, space, motion and sound include the software
program After-Effects, which has been described as Photoshop
for moving images. Other tools for creating dynamic titles, 3D
elements, special effects, character animation, organic camera
paths, image processing and composites include New Tek
Lightwave, Maxon Cinema 4D, 3D Studio Max, Maya, Motion, Final
Cut Pro and Soft Image XS1, digital cameras, scanners and of
course pencils and paper and the imagination to use them.

Designers, illustrators, animators and artists at the forefront of this
field include Pleix, Johnny Hardstaff, Tim Hope, Shynola, Light
Surgeons, Graphickers, Tomato, Attik, Geoff McFetridge, Tanaka
Noriyuki, Furifuri, Geoffroy de Crecy, Psyop, Tanaka Hideyuki,
Power Graphixx, UVA, Richard Kenworthy, Fuel, Intro, Mike Mills,
Michel Gondry, Momoco, Olivier Kuntzel and Florence Deygas,
Chris Cunningham and Spike Jonze.

Related information

Information such as historical
precedents and term definitions
are also included.

NARRATIVE STRATEGIES

'I never use models or nature for the figure, drapery or anything else.' Sir John Tenniel

The strategies and methodologies to create visual narratives vary, working processes include experimental and intuitive approaches as in collage, abstract and expressive imagery generated by the imagination. Alternatively, narratives can be crafted by integrating observational life drawing, reportage (on-the-spot drawing), the use of photographic reference or drawing from television and DVDs.

When constructing a story from reportage it is advisable to sketch rapidly while really looking and thinking about your subject matter, such as people, animals, objects and their location.

Observe the way they interact and react to one another and determine the motivations of your characters.

In order to develop a plot from the scene you are observing you will need to be able to empathise with the characters you are drawing and express their emotions and characteristics.

When visualising narrative either written by you or by another, it is important to keep in mind the message that is being transmitted, who the message is aimed at and its intention and audience.

Narratives can be set in many contexts – historical, contemporary, mythological and futuristic – therefore appropriate research will enhance the realism, detail and continuity of your images.

Build your own archive or library of imagery and make use of Internet search engines, your own photographic or video reference, found images, libraries, car boot sales, auctions, flea markets and charity shops. All this will provide visual reference material that can inform your work or trigger associations. You need to ensure that your illustrations are appropriate to the spirit of the story and be sensitive to the beat and rhythm of words and sentences.

'FRANCIS ROVE – IS ALL RIGHT' (opposite and overleaf)

Fantastical road-trip comic book series by Dennis Eriksson © 2006

FRANCIS ROVE ® – AUTO HOLIDAY is published by Stop-ill Publishing. Created by Dennis Eriksson, Stockholm, Sweden.

Description:
Various pages from
'Francis Rove' by
illustrator Dennis Eriksson

Thinking Sequentially

Draughtsmanship, craft skills and technical facility with a broad range of media will give you the flexibility to select the appropriate medium for the project. The illustrator can either be seen as collaborating or competing with the author, while amplifying and extending the subject matter.

A thorough reading and re-reading of the story or script and note taking will complement your visual research. Sequential images are constructed by looking, feeling and thinking.

When generating 'on the spot' drawings to develop a narrative you will become aware of factors such as the time of day, the height of the sun or the position of any other light sources and their effects, for example, chiaroscuro or ambient lighting. Be aware of the weather conditions, shadows, reflections, sounds, stillness, movement and action.

'The quality of an artist's comment is what is appreciated by the discriminating editor or art director. A subjective, intensely personal interpretation gives an extra dimension to the printed page, giving it the kind of dramatic edge that the camera finds difficult to equal.' Paul Hogarth, *Creative Pencil Drawing*, 1964, Studio Vista, London

'If you could...' at the V&A Village Fête 2006 (Right)

'If you could' is an annual publication set up by designers Will Hudson and Alex Bec, aiming to showcase the best in design and illustration around the idea, 'If you could do anything tomorrow, what would it be?'. Each publication is launched alongside an exhibition showing every single contribution received, meaning nobody's work goes unseen.

SEQUENTIAL IMAGES: NARRATIVE STRATEGIES

Orchestrating a Sequence

It is important to establish the mood and atmosphere of the story. This can be achieved by manipulating the point of view, eye level or eye path of the reader and by the use of close ups, extreme close ups, medium shots, long shots, extreme long shots and high, low and tilted angles. Also be aware of the body language of your characters. Their gestures, facial expressions and their relationship to one another and to objects and their location are extremely important.

Orchestrating a sequence of drawings can also involve the use of design elements, such as visual metaphors, symbolism, resonance and reverberation in order to inject emotions and wit. Some visual narratives, such as Frans Masereel's novels without words, interpret text without the use of typography, however, many illustrated narratives also integrate imagery with typography. The choice of letterform or font, its weight and legibility must be appropriate and harmonious to the spirit of the story, to the rhythm and style of the illustrations and to the overall design.

An example of Gillray's work – 'The Fall of Icarus' (Right)

Reproduction of an original 1807 etching by James Gillray.

Image courtesy of www.cartoonstock.com.

An example of Hogarth's work – 'The Rake's Progress' (Overleaf)

60 x 670 mm (37 13/16 x 26 3/8 in.) etching by William Hogarth.

Image courtesy of www.cartoonstock.com.

SEQUENTIAL IMAGES : NARRATIVE STRATEGIES

The FALL of ICARUS.

Crafting Visual Narratives

The selecting and editing of images is crucial, it is a matter of choosing images that capture essential moments and climaxes that highlight and communicate the narrative.

The manipulation of the picture plane, the foreground, middle ground, background, depth of field and the use of negative and positive space can also enhance visual communication.

The weaving of visual stories is all about the rhythm of images, flow, timing and the pace of the story. Illustrators are also concerned with the design of the sequence, characterisation, a sense of place, atmosphere, drama, the use of white space and allowing the pictures to breathe.

There are many commonalities and overlaps within the disciplines of film, animation, game design, comics and book illustration and each area can and has influenced the other.

Quick and direct drawing enables you to work up your idea or underlying theme and develop your perceptual skills. Pictorial storytelling is both a conceptual and intuitive process as formal elements, content, context and meaning are all explored and manipulated.

Sequential image-makers can make use of all the formal elements of drawing and design, such as weight and sensitivity of line, use of colour and tone, composition, shape, repetition, texture, mass, analogy, perspective, balance and hierarchy, scale and contrast.

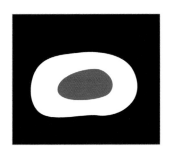

Airside – 'Cyclops' Storyboard (1)

A still for an animated ringtone sequence about a cute, but destructive laser-eyed cyclops for Panasonic Mobile, Japan.

Airside – 'Hand' Storyboard (2)

A still for an animated ringtone sequence about the perils of being the hand while playing ball for Panasonic Mobile, Japan.

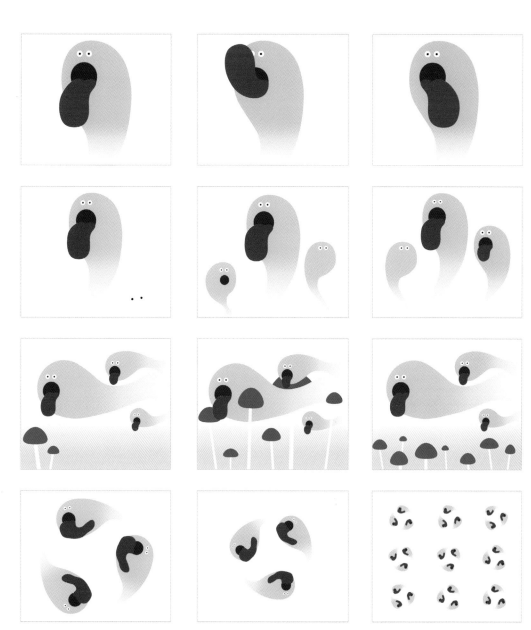

Airside – 'Ghost' Storyboard (3)

A still for an animated ringtone sequence about a mysterious group of playful ghosts for Panasonic Mobile, Japan.

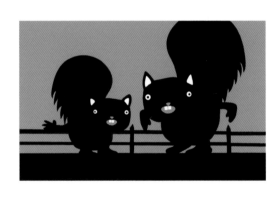

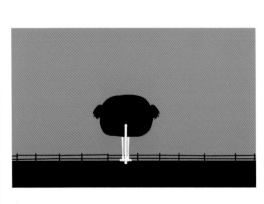

Urban music to your phone,
with Orange World

Soul to your phone,
with Orange World

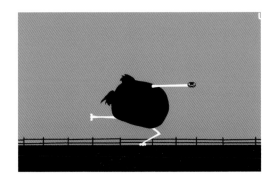

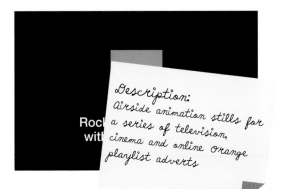

Roc
wit

Description:
Airside animation stills for
a series of television,
cinema and online Orange
playlist adverts

Description:
Scenes from a series of
MTV 'idents' combining
previously filmed video
footage and added animated
characters by Airside

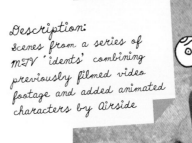

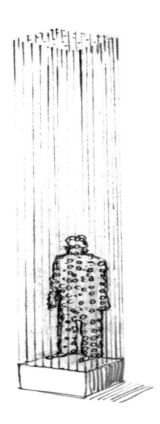
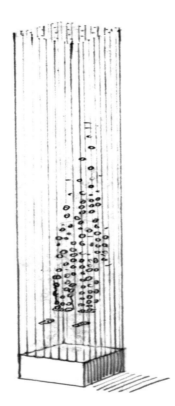
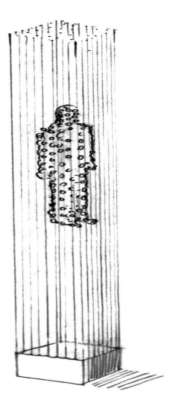

Description:
Sketches produced at the
beginning of the Source
project to describe the idea
of the installation

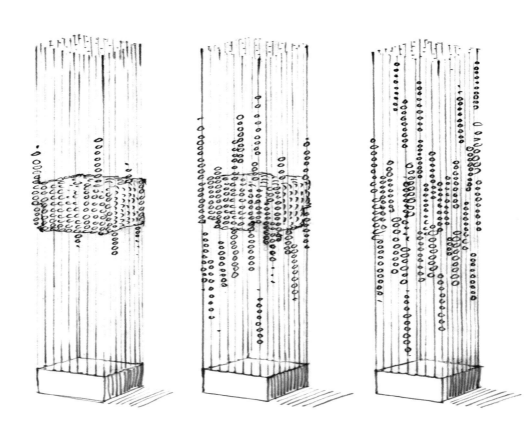

Greyworld – 'Source' project

Greyworld's interactive projects include a permanent installation at the London Stock Exchange, which opens the UK markets every morning at 8am and is broadcast to an estimated global audience of 80 million people. The artwork is formed from a grid of cables, arranged in a square, 162 cables in all, reaching eight storeys into the roof. Nine spheres are mounted on each cable and are free to move independently up and down its length. In essence the spheres act like animated pixels, able to model any shape in three dimensions – a fluid, dynamic, three-dimensional television.

Description:
The Greyworld Source project installation 'starting up' at the London Stock Exchange

Description:
Computer test models and details of the Greyworld Source project installation relaying the day's news

Visual Grammar

Design elements must be co-ordinated into a whole, combining balance and harmony with variety and the unexpected in order to avoid monotony.

Diversity and vitality can be achieved by exploiting the vertical or horizontal formats of pages and the flow and positions of images, for example, the use of margins, gutters, page bleed, double-page spreads, spots, half pages, full pages, vignettes and panels.

Illustrators control the use of visual grammar and play with syntax as they craft narratives that enable readers/viewers to identify and empathise with characters and dramatic situations.

The portrayal of psychological factors and the heightening of dramatic tensions in a narrative can also be achieved by the use of silhouettes, lighting, focus, the cropping, overlapping and linking of images, foreshortening and exaggeration, the forcing of perspective and the use of dramatic angles.

The Peepshow Collective (Right)

The Peepshow Collective is not so much about safety in numbers, but eclectic methodology and offers ideas that draw upon the experience and individual, as well as group skills. The Peepshow Collective is: Luke Best, Jenny Bowers, Miles Donovan, Chrissie MacDonald, Pete Mellor, Marie O'Connor, Andrew Rae, Elliot Thoburn, Lucy Vigrass and Spencer Wilson to date.

The Incredible Stunt

Nike 'Joga'

SEQUENTIAL IMAGES: NARRATIVE STRATEGIES

The Peepshow Collective (continued from previous page)

Stills from animated shorts *The Incredible Stunt* and *Colour*, together with an animation for the Nike *Joga Bonito* campaign.

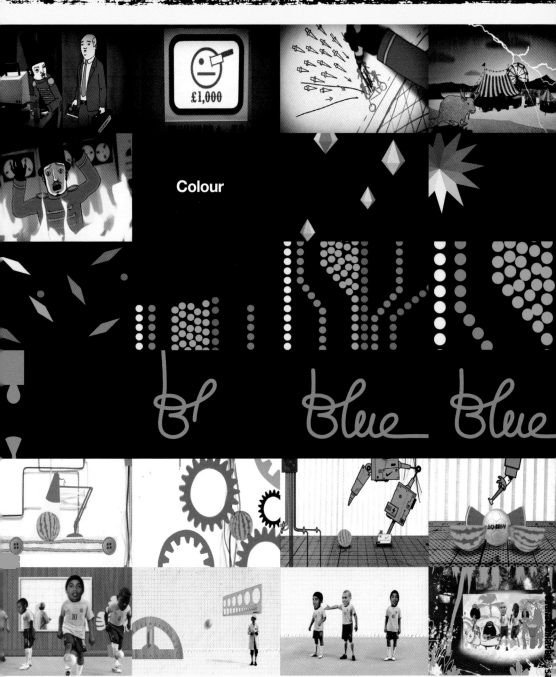

Colour

Storyboards

The storyboard is a key tool of visual communication and is used in many contexts to pre-visualise projects, such as business (group brainstorming), advertising agencies to plan campaigns, animation, motion graphics, interactive media, websites (such as sitemaps, navigation links), product design, film and theatrical productions.

The early use of storyboards can be traced back to animator Webb Smith's work at the Walt Disney studio of the 1930s and with the development of films such as *Steamboat Willie* (1928).

In the advertising context the storyboard artist operates as a freelancer employed by art directors and is described as a visualiser. Storyboards are often used to clearly pitch ideas to potential clients and assist art directors.

Contemporary illustrators create storyboards with a range of media from pencils, markers to graphics tablets, software and digital cameras. Some professionals now work with pre-drawn storyboard software that contains templates and allows video clips, still pictures and sounds to be imported. Non-linear editors are able to manipulate the sequence of the still images arranging frames to play with narrative elements and continuity.

In the field of animation, storyboards are developed into animatics, which act as moodboards in motion with still images that move to express the atmosphere and key points of the narrative with an accompanying initial soundtrack. Influential British animators John Halas and Joy Batchelor were noted for the visual scripting of all their films.

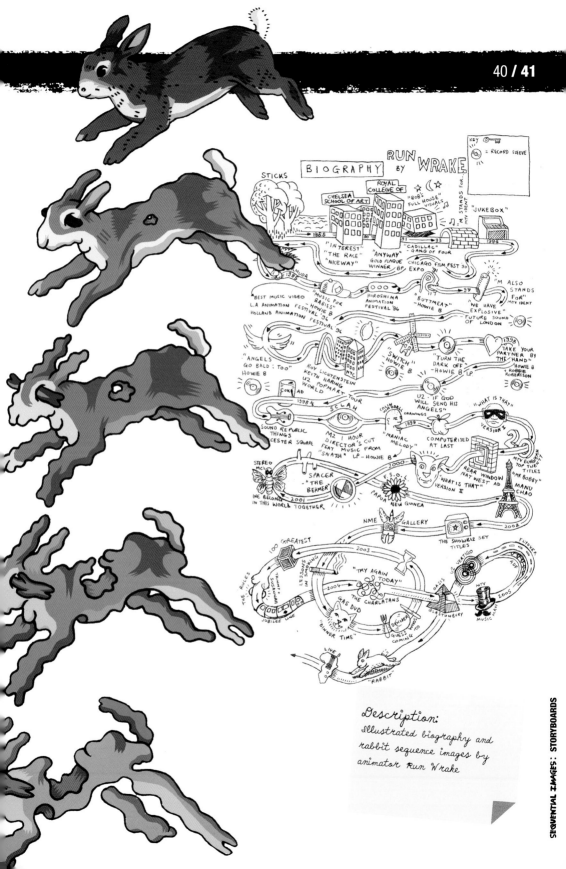

Description:
Illustrated biography and rabbit sequence images by animator Run Wrake

Description:
Hearts and Lub Heads. Pages from Run Wrake's sketchbooks, showing working drawings for animations

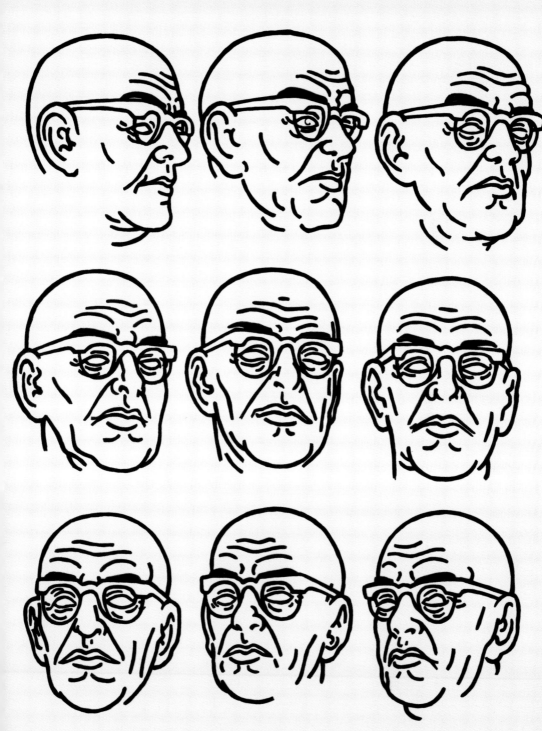

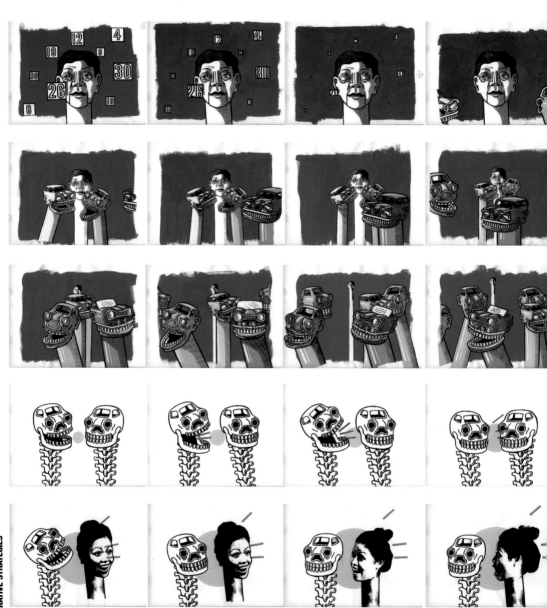

'Jukebox' © Run Wrake 1994 – Ten seconds of a five-minute animation

This early work features photocopied, hand drawn and painted images in a story, which when combined with the instrumental soul music of Curtis Mayfield's *Move On Up,* takes you on a epiphanic *'personal journey through fragmented experience'*. Made while still at college by anarchic UK illustrator and animator Run Wrake.

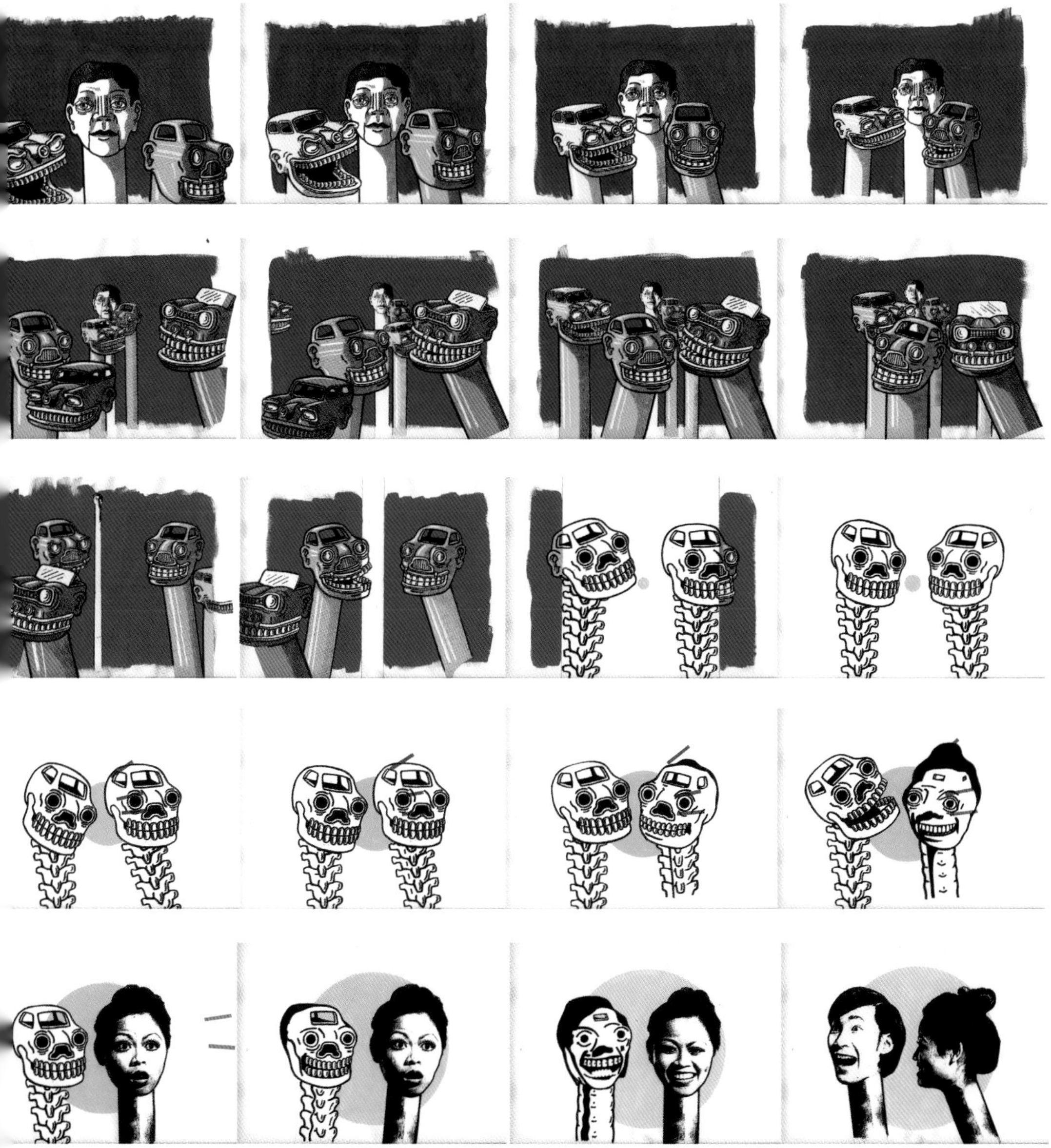

1. Microscopic close-up of moths wing

2. Moth sitting on abs

4. Magpie mosaic lining a motor way clogged
   with slow moving Morris Minors

5. Camera pulls back t

6. Milk float stranded on motor way

7. Previous shot actually
   flying Morse code 'm'

ic pattern

3. Moth on mosaic of magpie

e cab of a milk float, milkman inside studying a map with a magnifying glas

n a mirror held by macho moose wearing a medallion, flexing his muscles in front of music and surrounded by

8. Mouth closes over macho moose

9. Mouth belongs to a measles mumbling

10. Camera pulls back to reveal millions of monks

11. Monks form dot pat

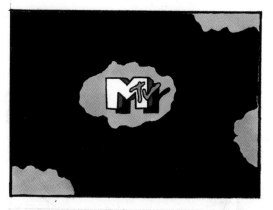

13. Logo recede, green background surrounded by abstract black

...ring monk with

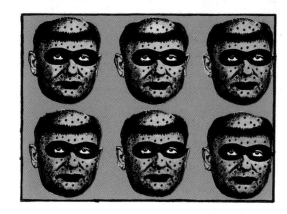

in turn. . . .

12. becomes drop shadow of MTV logo

Description:
The finished MTV
animation can be seen at
RunWrake.com under
TV graphics

14. Recession continues until logo too small to see,
      the loop is complete and we return to the beginning.

Film Design

A pictorial interpretation of a film requires draughtsmanship, speed and the creation of a visual script.

Some film directors draw their own storyboards. For example, Ridley Scott is known for his extensive use of rough sketches that capture all the shots of his films as are Joel and Ethan Coen for films such as *Fargo, Miller's Crossing* and *The Big Lebowski*.

In the film industry art directors, production designers and scenic artists have always played a vital role. Part book illustrator part architect, production designers create drawings that visualise ideas, emotional content and dramatic action and are interpreted by directors, set dressers and cinematographers.

The film *The Cabinet of Dr. Caligari* (1919), directed by Robert Wiene featured atmospheric and distorted set design.

The designers of the film, Walter Röhrig and Hermann Warm, were associated with the Berlin Sturm group and drew on imaginative expressionism. Warm felt that 'films must be drawings brought to life'.

The film's themes of fantasy, horror and romance were interpreted through distorted windows, rooftops, curved walls and angles. The design transmitted the psychological effect of its subject matter to its audience and proved highly influential.

Soviet film-maker Sergei Eisenstein made use of storyboards constructing his montage films, which emphasised the importance of relating the form of the film to its meaning.

Description:
'How to avoid disaster'
by London-based
illustrator
Frazer Hudson

Art Direction

Innovative use of art direction and design can also be seen in the films of Fritz Lang in Germany, Cavalcanti in France and Sir Alexander Korda who came from Hungary to London via Paris.

The design of British films was enhanced in the 1920s and 1930s by the arrival in the UK of designers such as Vincent Korda (brother of Alexander), Alfred Junge, Erno Metzener, Oscar Werndorff, Lazar Meerson, André Andrejew and Ferdinand Bellan.

Alfred Junge was responsible for the visual design of films such as *Colonel Blimp*, *A Matter of Life and Death* and *Black Narcissus* for Archers Film Productions. Andre Andrejew's drawings were influenced by the work of Gustave Doré, he art directed in Germany, France and England designing sets for Duvivier's *Golem* and Pabst's *Dreigroschenoper* in 1931.

Many of these art directors were firm believers in the future of film as an art form. Hein Heckroth, who designed sets and costumes for theatre, ballet and film, including Michael Powell's *The Red Shoes,* stated that *'all the machinery and all the money in the world will not help to make a good production if you have nothing to say – no idea'.*

Key figures include Ralph Brinton for the design of Carol Reed's *Odd Man Out*, 1946, Norman Arnold for *Hue and Cry* by Ealing Studios, Wilfred Arnold's backgrounds for Alfred Hitchcock's *Blackmail*, Roy Oxley's designs for Sidney Gilliat's *London Belongs to Me*, Lawrence Paul Williams's work on *Brief Encounter*, and production designer William Cameron Menzies storyboarding for *Gone with the Wind*, 1939.

All these designers were able to visualise and interpret stories creating effective, intelligent and lyrical illustrations to highlight the mood, visual rhythm, lighting, background, costumes and architectural planning of scenes.

John Bryan, the designer for *Oliver Twist* and *Great Expectations*, felt that *'a film consists of a series of two-dimensional illustrations in movement thereby introducing a third dimension. The design, therefore, becomes three-dimensional and in essence largely a planning problem.'* Art and Design in the British Film, Edward Carrick, 1948

SEQUENTIAL IMAGES: NARRATIVE STRATEGIES

Description:
Ed gill aka 'the koolest
artist' (Art Director) with
his spray and bubble
machines. Photographed
by Ali Peck

Obliquity and Anti-narrative

Cultural factors are paramount, whether the image is created as a supposedly neutral example of information design or as persuasive visual rhetoric or entertainment. Coherent communication, traditions, conventions and parameters are often subverted in the arts.

'Isn't life a series of images that change as they repeat themselves?' Andy Warhol

The viewer/reader is often made to work to decode visual messages and texts. Complex, experimental and subversive approaches to narrative can be seen in the work of many illustrators, poets, architects, authors, playwrights, animators, choreographers, musicians, designers, photographers, artists and film directors. In-depth research feeds the personal growth of the illustrator and broadens discourse by relating your work to other practitioners.

Research image-makers' points of view, analyse their careers, inspirations, working processes, philosophies and cultural significance. The challenging and influential work of the following storytellers from a myriad of disciplines can provide the sequential image-maker with a rich source of inspiration:

Jean-Luc Godard, David Lynch, Luis Buñuel, Quentin Tarantino, Akira Kurosawa, Andrei Tarkovsky, Alfred Hitchcock, Stanley Kubrick, Samuel Beckett, Harold Pinter, William Burroughs, Kurt Vonnegut, James Joyce, Dylan Thomas, Jorge Luis Borges, Isaac Asimov, Philip K. Dick, Patti Smith, Haruki Murakami, Franz Kafka, John Cooper Clark, FT Marinetti, Hayao Miyazaki, Gertrude Stein, David Lean, François Truffaut, Jean Cocteau, Sergei Eisenstein, John Huston, Henry Darger, Frank Capra, John Ford, Orson Welles, William Shakespeare, Buster Keaton, Mervyn Peake, Beatrix Potter, Billie Holiday, Norman McLaren, Martin Parr, Adolf Wolfi, Hans Christian Andersen, Tom Waits, Jim Jarmusch, Jacques Tati, Martin Scorsese, Robert Weaver, Saul Steinberg, Eva Hesse, John Carpenter, Nic Roeg, Werner Herzog, Wim Wenders, Federico Fellini, Grandma Moses, Edward Gorey, Matt Groening, Henri Cartier Bresson, Diane Arbus, Albert Camus, Wong Kar Wai, Robert Crumb, Jacques Brel, Nick Cave, Edith Piaf, Dieter Roth, Edgar Allan Poe, D.W. Griffith, Michelangelo Antonioni, Stéphane Mallarmé, Frida Kahlo and Pier Paolo Pasolini.

Description:
Ed Gill, aka 'the Koolest
Artist', in the studio
making a skeleton art
film. Photographed by
Cedric Gatillon

WIG OUT

© MARK WIGAN 2003

Description:
One of the many pictorial storytelling books illustrated by the author

PICTORIAL STORYTELLING

Graphic art and pictorial storytelling has a long and rich history that can be traced back to the cave paintings of Altamira and Lascaux, Egyptian hieroglyphics, Mayan, Aztec, Greek, Persian and Roman manuscripts.

Antecedents and precursors of today's narrative illustration can be found in artefacts such as Trajan's Column in Rome AD 113, medieval illuminated manuscripts to the Bayeux Tapestry (circa AD 1100), Michelangelo's Sistine Chapel, the narrative paintings of Brueghel and Bosch, the woodcuts of Dürer, Japanese woodblock prints, allegory, emblems, rebus puzzle books, 16th-century broadsheets and 17th-century chap books sold by peddlers.

The use of wood engraving, etching and lithography in the 18th century opened the way for production of outstanding books, such as Thomas Bewick's *General History of Quadrupeds*, the aquatint etchings of Francisco de Goya and the idiosyncratic book art of William Blake.

The publishing of sequences of prints and the introduction of what we consider comic book conventions, such as speech balloons, labels and frames, appeared in the works of English biting graphic satirists William Hogarth, Thomas Rowlandson, George Cruickshank, Richard Doyle and James Gillray.

The invention of the comic book itself has been credited to Swiss artist Rodolphe Töpffer around 1830 to 1840. He drew his characters in panels for satirical and humorous picture books, such as *Histoire de Mr. Jabot* (1835) and *Monsieur Pencil* (1840).

Narrative prints appeared in story papers, such as *Le Charivari* (1832), featuring the incisive works of Honoré Daumier.

Highly influential were the publication of the *Illustrated London News* in 1842 and the popular fiction of the *Penny Dreadful*. Of note are *Boys of England* (1866), *Punch* (1841), *Life* (1883) and *Puck*, Keppler and Schwartzman's cartoon magazines of 1876. *Ally Sloper's Half Holiday*, by Gilbert Dalziel (1884), was a black-and-white weekly paper inspired by the music hall.

Other titles included *Comic Cuts* and the slapstick *Illustrated Chips* (half-penny comics).

A FAMILY TO FEED
OUT OF CONTROL
HURDY GURDY
CURIOUS
PSYCHOTI
YES
MICROBE EMISSARY
FAT RESERVES
SWIMS 100 KM NON STOP
MARAUDER
WHIMSICAL MESSENGER
ABSURD HULLABALOO!
MUTE
JUJU PLAYBOY ENVOY
ERRATIC
SWAMP MISCREANT

Description:
A sample spread from
'WigOut', illustrated
by Wigan

The World of Comics

R.F. Outcault's 'The Yellow Kid' became a popular syndicated cartoon in the 1890s and led to the production of licensed products, such as fans, badges, buttons, cigars and crackers.

The development of comic book innovation can be traced through from R.F. Outcault to strips such as Rudolf Dirk's *The Katzenjammer Kids*, George Herriman's *Krazy Kat*, Frederick Opper's *Happy Hooligan,* and Winsor McCay's *Little Nemo in Slumberland*. The most popular comic strip characters and stories were Harold Gray's *Little Orphan Annie*, Ernie Bushmiller's *Nancy*, Chester Gould's *Dick Tracy*, Chic Young's *Blondie*, Walt Kelly's *Pogo*, Wilson McCoy's *The Phantom*, Milton Caniff's *Steve Canyon*, Ham Fisher's *Joe Palooka*, Frank King's *Gasoline Alley*, Li'l Abner's *Al Capp*, E. C. Segar's *Popeye*, Carl Barks's *Donald Duck*, and *Beetle Bailey* by Mort Walker. Long running popular newspaper cartoon strips in the UK include *Andy Capp* by Reg Smythe (since 1957), *The Broons* by Dudley Watkins and Ken Harrison (1936–present), *Fred Basset* by Alex Graham (since 1963), *Modesty Blaise* by Peter O'Donnell, *Oor Wullie* by Dudley Watkins and Ken Harrison (1936–present), *The Perishers* by Maurice Dodd and Dennis Collins (1957–present), and *Rupert the Bear*, created by Mary Tourtel in 1920 and illustrated by Alfred Bestall between 1935 and 1965.

Comics address many genres and themes including biography, romance, reportage, horror, autobiography, journalism, essay, science fiction, westerns and crime. The comic book requires the interplay of text and image, the use of certain conventions, the fusion of reading, seeing and deciphering.

Comics are published either weekly or daily or online. Comics appear in newspapers as syndicated comic strips. They are also bound in albums, such as the hardback comics of *Tintin* and *Asterix*. Superhero comics remain popular and now have many film, TV and licensing spin offs. Marvel's big names are *Spider-Man*, *Thor*, *Hulk*, *Captain America* and the *Fantastic Four*, while DC Comics is responsible for *Superman* and *Batman*. Comics also appear as editorial illustrations, such as 'gag panels' and in the growing field of Japanese manga and full-length graphic novels. The cartoonist Will Eisner of *The Spirit* fame has been credited with producing the first graphic novel, *A Contract with God*, in 1978. Graphic novels are often being adapted into film, for example, Max Allan Collins's *Road to Perdition*, Dan Clowes's *Ghost World*, Frank Miller's *Sin City*, *Batman* and *300*, as well as *Men in Black*, *X-Men*, *Spider-Man*, *Superman*, *V for Vendetta* and *A History of Violence*.

Designosaurs by Scott Garrett

THAT "WHEEL" IDEA OF YOURS SURE WENT DOWN WELL WITH OUR PEOPLE.

I KNOW, BUT HOW WILL WE FOLLOW THAT UP?

WE ... WHAT DO YOU MEAN WE? ...THIS IS YOUR PROBLEM...WHAT DO I KNOW ABOUT DESIGN?

COME ON... I NEED SOME HELP ...YOUR "MONKEY WHACKER" WAS PRETTY COOL.

SURE WAS.

Designosaurs by Scott Garrett

Description:
An example of four weekly wry comic strips from the 'Independent' newspaper in the UK

SO THIS IS WHERE THE MAGIC HAPPENS..

A REAL CAULDRON OF ACTIVITY...THE NERVE CENTRE... FACTORY OF THOUGHT

SO ANY IDEAS?

NOPE. THE CURSE OF THE BLANK WALL

DON'T IDEAS GROW ON TREES?

NO. ANYWAY THE BIG FIRE BURNT ALL THE TREES.

DIDN'T YOU INVENT FIRE?

SHHHH!

Designosaurs by Scott Garrett

LET'S TAKE A WALK...CLEAR THE COBWEBS

IS THAT HOW YOU CAME UP WITH THE WHEEL?

NO. THAT CAME TO ME IN A DREAM

YOU GET "THE WHEEL" ..I GET NAKED LADIES...IT'S NOT FAIR!

Description:
A selection of 1960s' and 1970s' comics from the author's archive, including Marvel's 'Planet of the Apes'

MARCH 2ND 1973 GREAT JUNGLE ADVENTURES 6p

BY CANNIBALS!

FREE FULL COLOUR APES POSTER

LANET
APES

THE MOHOCK

FIRST COLLECTOR'S ITEM ISSUE:
BEGINNING -- AN ALL-NEW
ADAPTATION OF THE FIRST
GREATEST "APES" MOVIE!
NEVER BEFORE IN COMICS FORM!

ISSUE: THE WEDDING OF RE

THE MIGHTY WORLD OF

MARVE

STARRING THE INCREDIBLE

HULK

WEEK ENDING JULY 13, 1974

STOP STRUGGLING, GIRL!
THERE'S NOBODY GONNA
HELP YOU IN THE SLUM!

Alternative Comics

The alternative comics publishing industry is a direct descendant of the 1960s and 1970s underground comix movement. Leading publishers in the alternative field include Fantagraphics, Drawn and Quarterly, Top Shelf and High Water. Mini-comics, Web comics and 'zines are also a product of the do-it-yourself community.

The production of the idiosyncratic genre of mini-comics often requires the use of a long stapler, a photocopying machine, silk screen and a great deal of hard work. Outlets include alternative comics conventions, direct mail order or distribution via websites.

There is a number of alternative press conventions that showcase mini-comics; these include The Alternative Press Expo (APE) in San Francisco, USA, The Small Press and Alternative Comics Expo and the MoCCA Art Festival in New York. The largest comics convention is the San Diego Comic-Con, which is a huge comic book, video games, illustration, film and pop culture gathering.

The convention features costume competitions, and fans dress up as their favourite characters from films and anime. In Europe there is the large Angoulême International Comics Festival in France, which has been in existence since 1974 and is described as an international festival *de la Bande Dessinée*.

News reviews, interviews and commentary on the world of comics are supplied by many review sites, including Bug Powder, which promotes small-press self-published comics, Tom Spurgeon's informative blog The Comics Reporter, small-press comics emporium Optical Sloth and the industry bible *The Comics Journal*.

WUNDERLAND WAR

VINYL TOYS AND T-SHIRTS ABOUT CANDY AND GUNS

HORSE BITES

Description:
Poster for the alternative US shop Wunderland War by Horse Bites

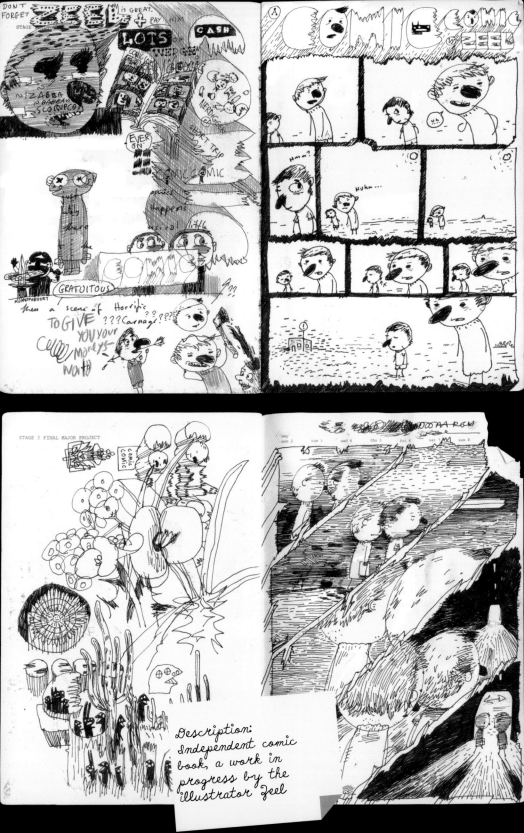

Description: Independent comic book, a work in progress by the illustrator Zeel

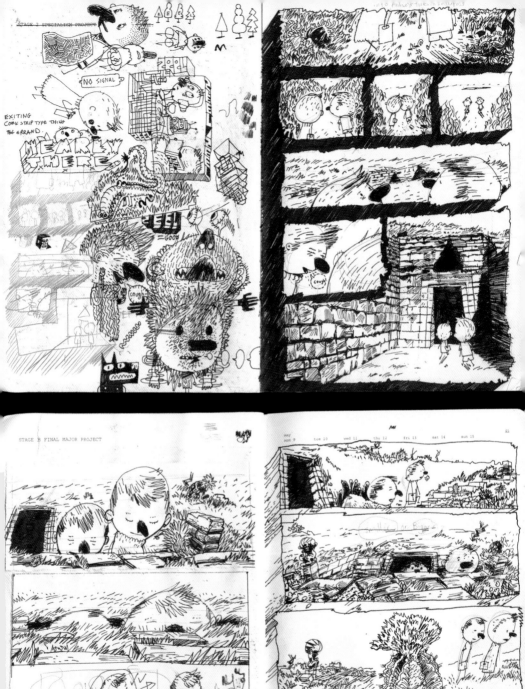

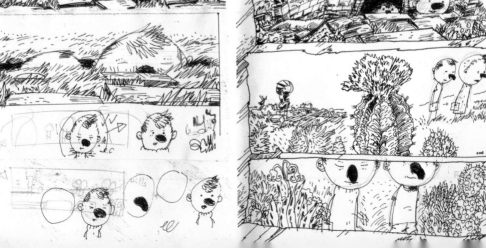

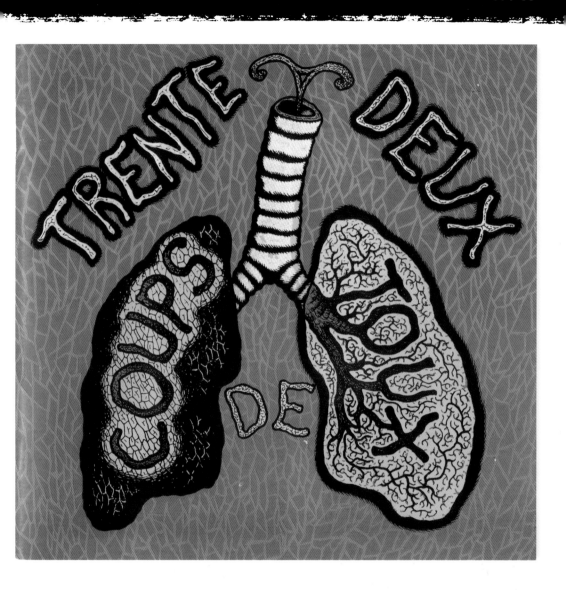

Description: (Left, top to bottom) 'Primitif' by Ed Pinsent, 'The Dial' by Chris Reynolds Publishers: Kingly Books

Artist:
Dr Marco Corona

Publisher:
Le Dernier Cri

Key Exemplars

If you plan on drawing your own comics, it's a good idea to research a diverse range of comic books for inspiration.

Key exemplars include:

Krazy Kat by George Herriman, *Arzach* and *Incal* by Jean 'Moebius' Giraud, *Peanuts* by Charles Schulz, *Maus* by Art Spiegelman, *Little Nemo in Slumberland* by Winsor McCay, *The Ganzfeld, Kramers Ergot, BLAB!, Donald Duck* by Carl Barks, *Eagle* by Frank Hampson, *Mad Comics* by Harvey Kurtzman & various, *Jimmy Corrigan: The Smartest Kid on Earth* by Chris Ware, *Barefoot Gen: The Day After* by Keiji Nakazaw, *The Adventures of Tintin* by Hergé, *Destiny* by Otto Nuckel, *The Spirit* by Will Eisner, *RAW* magazine edited by Art Spiegelman and Françoise Mouly, *The Acme Novelty Library* by Chris Ware, *Palestine* by Joe Sacco, *The Mishkin Saga* by Kim Deitch, *Delirius* by Philippe Druillet, *Locas* by Jaime Hernandez, *Akira* by Katsuhiro Otomo, *Beano* by Leo Baxendale, *Mad Man's Drum* by Lynd Ward, *99 Ways to Tell a Story* by Matt Madden, *Gasoline Alley* by Frank King, *Fantastic Four* by Jack Kirby and Stan Lee, *Sandman* by Neil Gaiman, *Plastic Man* by Jack Cole, *Sin City* by Frank Miller, *Tales from the Greenfuzz* by Will Sweeney, *Hell Baby* by Hideshi Hino, *Dick Tracy* by Chester Gould, *Passion eines Menschen* by Frans Masereel, *The Amazing Spider-Man* by Steve Ditko and Stan Lee, *Nausicaa of the Valley of the Wind* by Hayao Miyazaki, *The Kin-der-Kids* by Lyonel Feininger, *From Hell* by Alan Moore and Eddie Campbell, *Ghost World* by Daniel Clowes, *Amphigorey* by Edward Gorey, *V for Vendetta* by Alan Moore and David Lloyd, *Atom* by Osamu Tezuka, *The Dark Knight Returns* by Frank Miller, *Alec* stories of Eddie Campbell, *Optic Nerve* by Adrian Tomine, *It's a Good Life, If You Don't Weaken* by Seth, *A Contract with God* by Will Eisner, *The New Yorker* cartoons of Charles Addams, *Little Lulu* by John Stanley, *Eightball* by Dan Clowes, *Asterix the Gaul* by Albert Uderzo and René Goscinny, *American Splendor #1–10* by Harvey Pekar and various, *Little Orphan Annie* by Harold Gray, *Jimbo* by Gary Panter, *The Book of Jim* by Jim Woodring, *Black Hole* by Charles Burns, *Zap Comix* by Robert Crumb and various, *Persepolis II: The Story of a Return* by Marjane Satrapi, *Watchmen* by Alan Moore and Dave Gibbons, *Dennis the Menace* by Hank Ketcham, *The 9–11 Comic Strip* by Ernie Colon and Sid Jacobson, *World War 3 Illustrated* by Peter Kuper, and *Feiffer* and *Tantrum* by Jules Feiffer.

A broad range well worth further investigation.

Description:
Kramers Ergot #6 — The
leading avant-garde comix
anthology founded by
editor Sammy Harkham

Manga

The precursor of manga was 'Kibyoshi' satirical comics. The artist Kyoden made use of the term manga (whimsical or comic pictures) in his works of 1798.

Although contemporary manga can be seen as stemming from this tradition it has also been heavily influenced by western comics and animation. In Japan, visual storytelling can be traced back to 8th-century woodcuts, but it is the work of the Ukiyo-e school artists of the 18th and early 19th century that has proved the most influential to western art. Ukiyo-e means 'pictures of the floating world' and refers to work created during the Japanese Edo period of 1615 to 1868. Prints produced during this period came in the form of multicoloured printed broadsheets, woodblock-illustrated books and albums, printed board games, advertisements, lanterns, screens, fans, calendars, heroic triptychs, memorial prints and greeting cards. The content of the prints included the Kabuki Theatre, nature (for example, birds and flowers), landscapes, history, fables, erotica, myths and folklore. Leading artists included Hokusai, Hiroshige, Moronobu, Kuniyoshi, Harunobu, Kaigetsudo and Masanobu. Storytelling, the portrayal of people and the chronicling of events were a key concern for these artists.

With bold colours, rhythmic design and poetic use of sensuous line they captured the lives of actors, courtesans, wrestlers and heroes. Many western artists such as Degas, Manet, Van Gogh, Toulouse-Lautrec, Bonnard, Beardsley and the Beggarstaff Brothers were directly influenced by the prints from Japan.

Manga flows from the tradition of Ukiyo-e, Kibyoshi and western-style comic book drawing. After the Second World War, Japanese artists appropriated the large eyes and characteristics of the work of Walt Disney into their work. Manga is now a multi billion-dollar industry appealing to audiences around the world. Manga is often adapted into anime; the range of themes is immense from the humorous to the violent and sexually explicit. How-to-draw-manga books are very popular and the style has had a great influence on graphic storytelling all over the world (e.g. Nouvelle manga in France). Apart from the large anthology magazines that are produced in their thousands, there is also the alternative self-published small press manga known as Dojinshi, which also has its own outlets and conventions. Influential manga includes *Astro Boy* by Osama Tezuka, *Akira* by Katsuhiro Otomo, Hayao Miyazaki's epic *Nausicaa of the Valley of the Wind*, and Kazuo Koike and Goseki Kojima's *Lone Wolf and Cub*.

Manga genres and categories include: Redisu – Women, Seinen – Men, Shojo – Teenage girls, Shonen – Teenage boys, Gekiga – Dramatic pictures, Shojo-ai or Yuri – Lesbian romance, Shaonen-ai yaoi – Gay romance, and Hentai – Pornography.

Description:
Manga-inspired illustration for UK grimester's Roll Deep by illustrator Yuko Kondo

Tales from the Underground

The underground tradition can be traced through from the works of artists such as Bosch, Jacques Callot and Brueghel to William Hogarth's narrative series of engravings, William Blake's books, James Gillray's satirical cartoons, Gustave Doré, Grandville, Honoré Daumier's illustrations to George Herriman and Winsor McCay's comics.

In the 1930s and 1940s small booklets called the *Tijuana Bibles* or *Bluesies* were produced in their thousands. They featured satirical pornographic parodies of popular syndicated newspaper cartoon characters of their day. They made a significant contribution to the development of underground comics.

In the 1950s EC (Entertaining Comics) generated masses of lurid pulp comics such as *Weird Science*, *Tales from the Crypt* and *Frontline Combat*, inspired by science fiction and often drawing on the works of Edgar Allen Poe.

Cartoonists such as Harvey Kurtzman and Basil Wolverton defined the style of the absurd and satirical world of *Mad* magazine. The hippy counterculture spawned underground 'zines and comix, such as *East Village Other*, *Young Lust*, *Wimmens Comix*, *Zap Comics* and *The Fabulous Furry Freak Brothers*. Robert Crumb was at the forefront of this comic revolution with his characters such as Mr. Natural, Fritz the Cat and Angelfood Mc Spade. Alternative comic pioneers included: Wally Wood, Spain Rodriguez, S. Clay Wilson, Bill Griffith, Gilbert Shelton, Robert Williams, Lynda Barry, Rory Hayes and Rick Griffin.

RICARDO FLORES MAGÓN

(LI FEI

Description:
Work by Clifford
Harper, printed by
the Freedom Press in
London's East End

ANARCHISTS

A SET OF THIRTY-SIX
PICTURECARDS

ANARCHISTS

PORTRAITS BY
CLIFFORD HARPER

RUDOLPH ROCK

ANARCHISTS

A SERIES OF 36 CARD

LEO TOLS

Born 9 September 1828 Ya
Died 20 November 19

One of the greatest wr
Tolstoy was also a politic
though for a long time
term for himself due t
of violence. After y
experience of the C
travelled to Wester
Proudhon in 1861
He took the title
Peace for his most
of his teach

ANARCHISTS

A SERIES OF 36 CARDS : NUMBER 30

MAX STIRNER
HANN CASPAR SCHMIDT)

October 1806 Bayreuth, Germany
e 1856 Berlin, Germany

Stirner became a school
for girls in Berlin. Germany
highly unsuccessful
he remained
in extreme
r Ones',
his

STANLEY

MICHEL

JEAN VIGO

ÉLIS

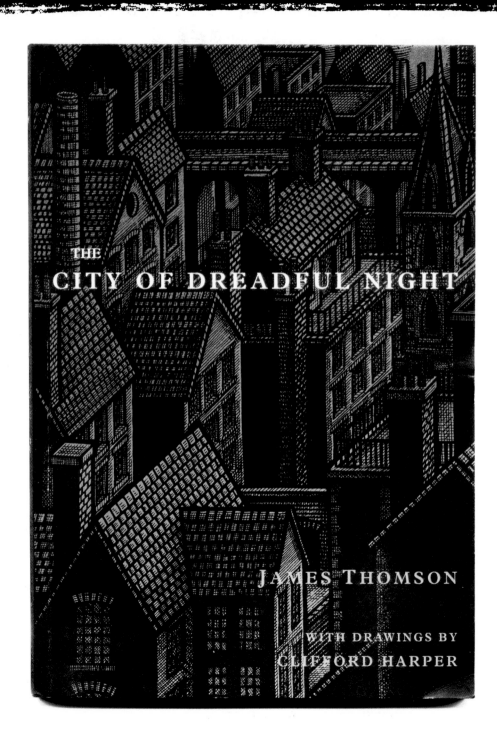

THE
CITY OF DREADFUL NIGHT

JAMES THOMSON

WITH DRAWINGS BY
CLIFFORD HARPER

SEQUENTIAL IMAGES: PICTORIAL STORYTELLING

In 1976, Gary Groth and Kim Thompson set up Fantagraphics Books featuring reprints of classic comics and showcasing leading-edge artists. During the 1980s a number of independent publishers, such as Knockabout Comics and Escape publishing in the UK, Raw Books and Graphics in the USA and Drawn and Quarterly in Canada promoted intelligent and alternative comics. *Raw* was established by Art Spiegleman and Françoise Mouly, its format was large, 11 x 14 inches, and within its pages were the works of leading avant-garde cartoonists such as Mark Beyer, Sue Coe, Charles Burns, Jacques Tardi and Gary Panter.

Escape magazine, like *Raw*, combined the work of 1960s underground comic artists with 1980s American and European work. Featured artists included Javier Mariscal, John Bagnall, Savage Pencil, Hunt Emerson and many more.

Fantagraphics Books have now become one of the leading publishers of innovative, alternative cartoonists' work. It has published the work of underground legend Robert Crumb, Gilbert and Jamie Hernandez, visual journalist Joe Sacco and Jessica Abel, whose work has received critical recognition for its personal themes, social relevance and experimentation. Amongst the leading anthologies of the present time are Fantagraphics *Blab!*, edited and designed by Monte Beauchamp. This annual is a showcase of fine art, illustration and comics, and within its pages are some of the world's leading contemporaries such as Johnathan Rosen, Gary Basemen, Clayton Brothers, Mark Ryden, Tim Biskup, Chris Ware and Dan Clowes.

The Ganzfeld is an annual book of pictures and prose, design, illustration, comics, picture stories and essays, which places them all in a historical and critical context. *The Ganzfeld* is edited by Dan Nadel, produced by PictureBox and published in association with the Gingko Press. Stories featured have included articles on the Hairy Who Art collective, the paintings of Brueghel, Deepspace photography, an illustrated essay by Alfred Hitchcock, as well as comic book history and theory. Featured artists have included Amy Lockhart, Peter Blegvad, Marc Bell and Julie Doucet.

From humble origins *Kramers Ergot* has grown to a massive 340-page flexi-bound anthology. The founding editor of this publication is cartoonist Sammy Harkham. It is packed with cutting-edge graphic narratives by Harkham himself, Vanessa Davis, Kevin Huizenga, Tom Gauld, Anders Nilsen, and David Lasky, to name but a few.

Description
An image from Spanish pop illustrator Rachel Ortas' 2005 'Ai Ai' children's book

ONCE UPON A TIME...

'They dined on mince and slices of quince, which they ate with a runcible spoon. And hand in hand on the edge of the sand, they danced by the light of the moon.' Edward Lear

Children's books are seen as mid- or long-term projects and are often written and illustrated by the same individual. The authorial voice requires the creation of a believable world, consistent and appealing characters, atmosphere, ideas and a union of words and images. The field values original and personal vision and provides freedom to experiment.

Maurice Sendak stated that his intention as an illustrator was *'to let the story speak for itself, with my pictures as a kind of background music – music in the right style and always in tune with the words.'* Illustrators of Children's Books, 1957–1966, ed. Lee Kingman

There are a wide variety of illustrated books aimed at children, fiction and non-fiction, picture books, novelty books, illustrated novels and tales, information and educational books.

Children's picture books are produced in a wide range of formats including plastic books with interactive tactile elements, pop-up books, pull-tab books, cloth books and board books. All elements of the design and construction of the books are considered in order to amplify the story in an appropriate way.

Elements such as binding, paper stock, format and paper engineering are taken into consideration. This attention to detail includes the appropriate placement of imagery and text to complement the flow of the narrative. By analysing the use of double-page spreads, duel image covers, end papers, flaps, wraparound covers, book covers, book formats and trim size we can see that all elements play a role.

Traditionally their purpose has been to entertain and educate, encouraging children to participate in narratives, which have often conveyed ideological, religious and moral messages, while employing charm, whimsy, nostalgia, fantasy, humour, pathos and fun. They embrace a wide range of themes including anthropomorphic tales, which deploy objects or animals as characters, fables, proverbs, poetry, nursery rhymes, folk tales, fairy tales, alphabet books and books to develop reading skills.

Publishing

Children's picture books are noted for their beautiful, sophisticated and colourful illustrations, which have been produced with various media and techniques, from the digital to cut-paper collage, sewing and quilting, watercolour, gouache, oil paint, pastels and pencils.

Illustrators create books in a wide range of visual languages, including work influenced by motifs from folk art or art brut, impressionism, expressionism, abstraction, surrealism, realistic styles or naive, comic and cartoon techniques.

The market for children's books is constantly growing with book projects expanding into animation, motion pictures, television series, toys, games and merchandise. The Bologna book fair is the world's largest gathering of children's publishing copyright professionals. Publishers representing over 60 countries display their latest products, negotiate licensing rights and view the portfolios of illustrators seeking book or multimedia deals.

Authors, illustrators, literary agents, TV/film producers, packagers, distributors, printers, book sellers and librarians meet to generate contacts, create new opportunities and buy and sell copyright. The book fair provides networking for illustrators to discuss film and broadcast rights, territories, royalty rights, and ethical issues. Portfolios are presented containing 'dummy books', evidence of plot development, character studies and a few pages of completed visuals. Publishers look for original and exciting imagery, strong ideas, design, consistent characterisation, draughtsmanship and stories that engage the imagination. It is essential that the illustrator researches a wide range of publishers, their target markets and international and cultural contexts.

Awards for excellence in the field of children's books include the Caldecott medal for the most distinguished picture book published in America, the Kate Greenaway medal for illustrators, the Macmillan book prize and the Biennial Illustration Bratislava.

Description:
Spreads from one of
Rachel Ortas' hand-
printed 'Ai Ai'
children's books

I CAN BITE YOU

100% eco friendly
rachelortas@hotmail.com

SEQUENTIAL IMAGES : PUBLISHING

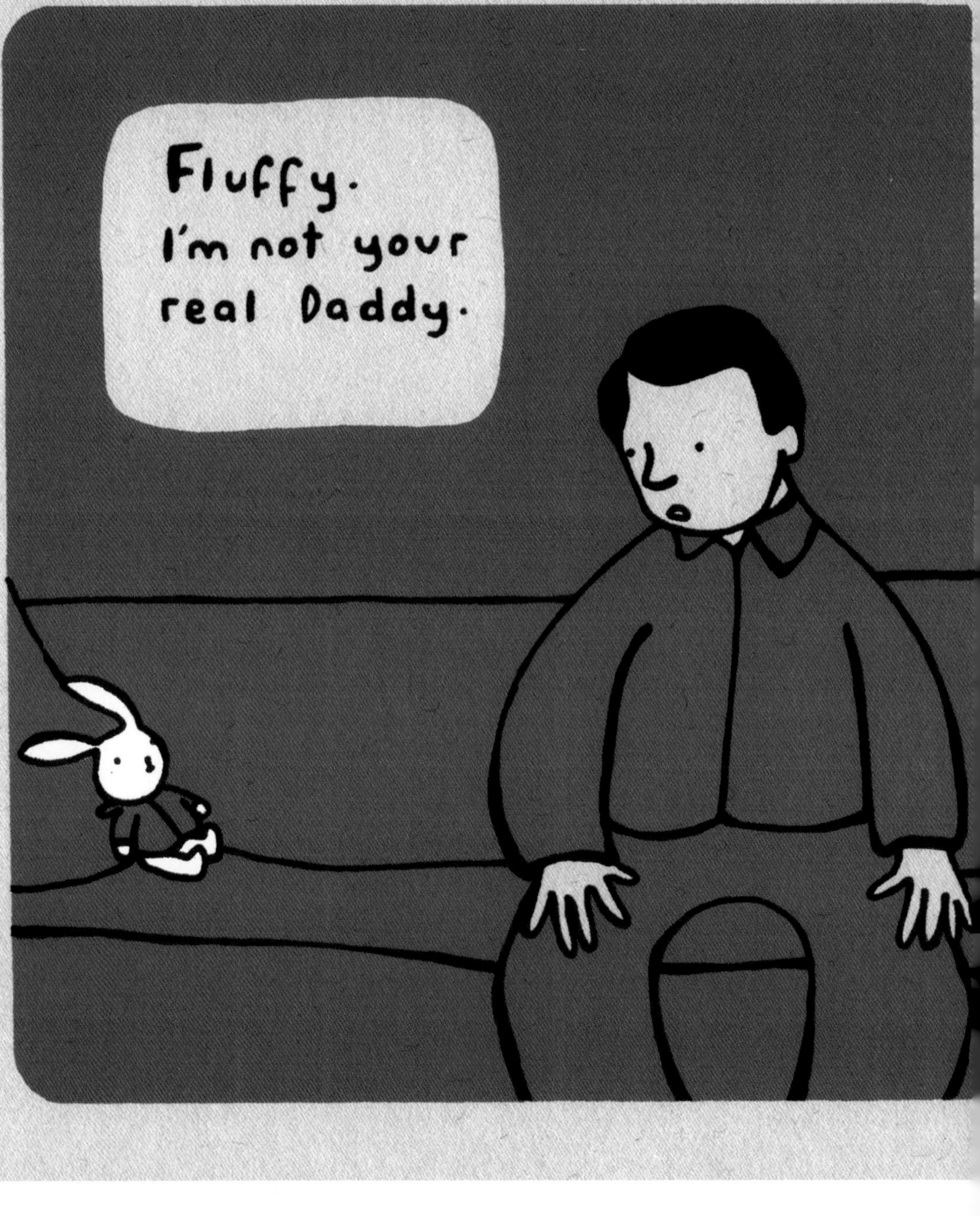
Fluffy.
I'm not your
real Daddy.

Description:
A limited edition
print from Simone
Lia's children's book
'Fluffy', published by
Cabanon Press

Yes you are Daddy.

Magical Works

'Sometimes I've believed as many as six impossible things before breakfast.'

Lewis Carroll

Research and discover the illustrators' motivations and attitudes, as well as their personal visual languages and techniques.

Sir John Tenniel's illustrations for Lewis Carroll's *Alice in Wonderland*, 1865

Edward Lear, *Book of Nonsense*, 1846

Arthur Rackham, *Fairy Tales of The Brothers Grimm*, 1900, *Rip Van Winkle*, 1905, *Peter Pan in Kensington Gardens*, 1906

Edmund Dulac, *Arabian Nights*, 1907

Stories from Hans Christian Andersen, 1911

The illustrated books of the Founder of the Brandywine School, Howard Pyle, such as

The Story of King Arthur and His Knights, 1903

Beatrix Potter's many books, including *The Tale of Peter Rabbit*, 1902

The illustrations of W. W. Denslow for *The Wonderful Wizard of Oz*, 1900

L. Lesley Brookes, *Ring O Roses*, 1922

E. H. Shepherd's illustrations for *Winnie the Pooh*, 1926

Jean de Brunhoff, *The Story of Barbar*, 1931

N. C. Wyeth, who illustrated the works of Robert Louis

Stevenson, *Treasure Island*, 1911, *Kidnapped*, 1913

The Story of Ferdinand written by Monro Leaf and illustrated by Robert Lawson, 1936

Curious George written and illustrated by H. A. Rey, 1941

Dr Seuss' *And to Think That I Saw It on Mulberry Street*, 1937

Dr Seuss' *Cat in the Hat*, 1957

Ludwig Bemelmans' *Madeline* books, 1939

Wanda Gag's *Millions of Cats*, 1928

Continued on page 87

Continued from page 84

Lois Lenski's *The Little Engine That Could*, 1930

Ida Rentoul Outhwaite's *Enchanted Forest*, 1921

Maxfield Parrish's *Arabian Nights*, 1909

Tove Jansson's *Moomin* stories, 1945

Dick Bruna's 115 *Miffy* (Nijntje) books, (since 1955)

A. B. Frost's *The Favorite Uncle Remus*, 1948

Maurice Sendak's *Where the Wild Things Are*, 1963

Quentin Blake's illustrations for the books of Roald Dahl (since 1975)

El Lissitzky, Constructivist children's books, 1920s

Antonio Frasconi's *See and Say* books, 1964

Pauline Baynes' *Lord of the Rings*, 1973

Alan Lee's *Faeries*, illustrated by Brian Froud, 1978

Paul Cox's *Abstract Alphabet*, 2001

Lane Smith, *The Stinky Cheese Man* by Jon Scieszka, 1986

Dr Heinrich Hoffmann's *Struwwelpeter* (*Shockheaded Peter*), 1846

Paula Metcalf's *Mabel's Magical Garden*, 2005

J. Otto Seibold's *Mr Lunch Takes a Plane Ride*, 1993

J. Otto Seibold's *Monkey Business*, 1995

Leading exemplars in the field of children's book illustration include: Charles Bennett, Richard Doyle, Bernard Boutet de Monvel, Edy Legrand, Cicely Barker, Mervyn Peake, Willie Pogany, Charles Keeping, John Lord, Leslie Brooke, Elsa Beskow, Edward Ardizzone, William Heath Robinson, Robert McCloskey, Helen Bannerman, Fritz Eichenberg, Edward Gorey, André François, Tomi Ungerer, Eric Carle, Alan Aldridge, Kveta Pacovska, Henrik Drescher, Frédérique Bertrand, Emma Chichester Clark, Anthony Browne, Mini Grey, Robin Harris, Tony Ross, Michael Foreman, Posy Simmonds, Raymond Briggs, Patrick Benson, Bruno Munari, Gro Dahle, Svein Nyhus, Sara Fanelli, J. Otto Seibold, Tim Burton, Stian Hole, Oyvind Torseter and Fam Ekman.

'Alice in Wonderland' (left and previous page)

Reproduction of the original illustrations by Sir John Tenniel for Lewis Carroll's *Alice in Wonderland*, 1865.

Images courtesy of www.cartoonstock.com.

SEQUENTIAL IMAGES : IMPORTANT WORKS

World of Wonder
Excitingly illustrated in full colour!

Growing up in the 1960s, I was an avid reader of richly illustrated educational magazines, such as *Look and Learn*, *Tell Me Why* and *World of Wonder*. Publishers such as Paul Hamlyn and Fleetway Publications Limited engaged their young audiences with themes such as *Clothes Through the Ages*, *The Bible Story*, *Man on the Move*, *World of Art*, *Population Charts*, *Maps* and *The Machine Age*. Illustrators such as Roger Barcilon, Giovanni Giannini and Michael Codd vividly interpreted famous battles of world history. Uniforms, arms, equipment, guns, ships, aircraft and methods of combat were all graphically depicted. In the 1970s my bedroom walls were plastered with illustrated posters; the organic landscapes of Roger Dean, Pauline Baynes' map of middle earth and fold-out posters from magazines such as *Science Fiction Monthly*, *The History of the Twentieth Century* and reprints of Second World War propaganda posters from the Imperial War Museum.

I would spend hours immersed in illustrated encyclopaedias creating my own imaginary narratives from looking at the work of illustrators, such as Zdenek Burian, whose wonderful illustrations were published by Paul Hamlyn in the UK in the 1960s. Burian illustrated over 500 books and articles and is familiar to children in the UK through titles such as *Prehistoric Animals* and *Prehistoric Man*.

My imagination was also fed by Ladybird books, which were sold in their millions worldwide and have been translated into 60 languages. The books have featured the work of many outstanding illustrators, including Harry Wingfield, Martin Aitchison and Frank Hampson – the creator of *Dan Dare Pilot of the Future* for the *Eagle* (1950–1959).

My favourite books were *The Adventures from History* series, which featured 49 titles including *William the Conqueror*, *Alfred the Great*, *Nelson*, *Stone Age Man In Britain* and *Robert the Bruce*. Many of them were illustrated by John Kenney who also illustrated *The Railway* series, later known as *Thomas the Tank Engine and Friends*, written by the Reverend W. Audry (1957–1962). Like many children I was enthralled by *The Tales of Rupert the Bear*, who had first appeared in the *Daily Express* in the 1920s, created by Mary Tourtel. Each Christmas I looked forward to the arrival of a *Rupert* annual featuring the illustrations of Alfred Bestall whose drawings were inspired by the landscape of his home in Snowdonia, Wales.

An early obsession with drawing battle scenes was triggered by the illustrations featured on the packaging of the products of the British toy manufacturer Airfix. Boxed plastic scale model kits contained illustrated construction diagrams and transfers. Airfix also produced 1:76-, 1:72-, 1:32-scale polythene model soldiers that were often customised using tins of Humbrol paint and sable brushes. Little armies of Romans, ancient Britons, the First World War, the Second World War, the American Civil War and characters such as astronauts, Robin Hood and his merry men and wagon train cowboys and Indians were painted and deployed in dioramas or war games.

Description:
The author and his
brother (left of Rocket) at
Sir John Deane's grammar
school for boys in
Northwich, 1970

By
T. HULES
S. BURRAGE
P. EMMERSON

Golden Years

'Keep open the imagination's supply lines to the past but do not turn away from the present.' Robert Hewison

The *Orbis Sensualium Pictus* (*The Visible World in Pictures*), by Johannes Amos Comenius from 1658 is recognised as the first children's picture book. Developments in education and in the printing of books (for example, the transition from gravure to colour lithography) initiated the creation of the richly illustrated books of the late 19th century and early 20th century.

In England, illustrators created a nostalgic view of childhood and drew influences from Japanese prints, the Arts and Crafts Movement and the Pre-Raphaelites.

Exemplars include English illustrators Walter Crane, Kate Greenaway and Randolph Caldecott (described as the lord of the nursery) and their books produced with printer Edmund Evans. In the USA, Howard Pyle and his Brandywine School of Illustrators, such as N.C. Wyeth, Jessie Wilcox Smith, Harvey Dunn and Maxfield Parrish produced lavishly painted illustrations for children's literature.

Howard Pyle established his own school of art and illustration, selecting students to live and work at his home and studio. He described his criteria for selecting students in 1900 as this: *'I shall make it a requisite that the pupils whom I choose shall possess first of all imagination, secondly artistic ability, thirdly colour and drawing and I shall probably not accept any who are deficient in any one of these three requisites.'* Letter to Edward Penfield, quoted in *The Illustrator's Notebook*, ed. Lee Kingman, 1978

The children's books produced in the Soviet Union in the 1920s and early 1930s featuring the work of illustrators such as V. V. Lebedev became highly influential in this genre. Books from the Golden Age of illustration have become highly sought after collector's items due to their 'nostalgic qualities', high production values and beautiful illustrations.

'Learning the Polka' (right)

Learning the Polka by John Leech for *Punch* magazine.

Images courtesy of www.cartoonstock.com.

THE POLKA

1. My Polka before Six Lessons. 2. My Polka after Six Lessons.

Characters
Gotta catch 'em all!

We are bombarded by characters, in books, films, TV and on the Internet. New characters are constantly being launched from images posted on blogs and websites, including online e-games, e-comics and e-animation.

The World Wide Web generates character phenomena and celebrities, for example, Dancing Baby, Chicken Costumes, Crazy Frog, Ultimate Showdown of Ultimate Destiny, and Hamster Dance.

All manner of weird and wonderful characters are being self-published. Illustrated characters are disseminated into many media, often becoming the products of merchandising and branding, for example, featured on T-shirts, e-flyers, badges, stickers, posters, mugs, mouse mats, games, sew-on patches, USB keys, mobile phones, iPods and toys.

Our imaginations are populated by characters from our earliest years. Just a few off the top of my head include Alice, the Mad Hatter, Tweedle Dee

Description: (here and next page)
Vinyl toy characters and Star Wars merchandise by the illustrator known as JAKe

Description: (left)
A selection of handmade limited edition plush toy characters by illustrator Rosie Short

and Tweedle Dum, Humpty Dumpty, the Cheshire Cat, Teletubbies, Mickey Mouse, the Yellow Kid, Peter Rabbit, Jeremy Fisher, Squirrel Nutkin, Jemima Puddleduck, Mrs Tiggywinkle, Kermit the Frog, Snoopy, Bugs Bunny, Daffy Duck, Felix the Cat, Astroboy, Toad of Toad Hall, Fungus the Bogeyman, Dougal and Zebedee, Bungle and Zippy, Yogi Bear, Big Bird, Ren and Stimpy, Tom and Jerry, Cobi, Muffin the Mule, Korky the Cat, Troy Tempest and Mike Mercury, King Kong, Superman, Tintin, The Incredible Hulk, Godzilla, Pekochan, Marukome kun, Pokémon, Devil Robots, R2D2, The Scream, Ultraman, Olive the Reindeer, Bibendum, Mr Magoo, Mr Benn, Mr Men, the Seven Dwarfs, Desperate Dan, the Amazing Spider-Man, Popeye, Olive Oil, Pooh, Betty Boop, Fritz the Cat, Crazy Frog, Pinocchio, Captain Scarlet, PacMan, Joe 90, Dennis the Menace, Miffy, Mighty Mouse, ET, Sof' Boy, Road Runner, Taz, Super Mario Brothers, Buzz Lightyear, Top Cat, Bart Simpson, Mr Natural, Roobarb, Cat in the Hat, Giles Family, Noddy, Gerald McBoing-Boing, Big Ears, Krazy Kat and Ignatz, the Wombles, Bill and Ben, Hello Kitty, Quick Draw McGraw, Penelope Pitstop, Huckleberry Hound, Deputy Dawg, Dick Dastardly and Mutley, Hair Bear Bunch, Hong Kong Phooey, Touche Turtle and Wally Gator, Secret Squirrel and Morocco Mole, Itchy and Scratchy, and Krusty the Clown.

SEQUENTIAL IMAGES : CHARACTERS

Description:
Ronzo's Jonny-Fu
plush toy takes a trip
to Japan on a
promotional tour

NEIGHBORS

AN ACADEMY AWARD FILM

Norman McLaren's famous film parable, made without words to show all people the futility of violence for settling quarrels.

The story, told entirely in the action, concerns two men who live tolerantly beside each other until one day a flower emerges on the borderline between their properties.

At first they share the beauty of the flower, but when each desires the flower for himself a violent struggle begins. The unrestrained savagery of angry men gains shattering force by McLaren's use of animation principles to give the movements of his actors a speed and power far larger than life. Their feet barely skim the ground as they flash by in attack and pursuit. One man, with a wave of his hand, erects a fence; the other, with one gesture, flattens the barrier.

Peace comes only when the men, their families and their homes are utterly destroyed. Then, on two quiet graves, each neat and equal, a flower grows. A multilingual title, "Love Thy Neighbor", concludes the film.

Accompanying sound was produced by the film artist, without recourse to instruments other than those needed to draw sound-making patterns for the soundtrack.

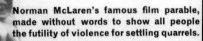

Production and Animation........ Norman McLaren
Acting ....Jean-Paul Ladouceur
                                         Grant Munro
Photography .... Wolf Koenig

16mm & 35mm   Color or Black & White
Running Time: 9 minutes

Produced by THE NATIONAL FILM BOARD OF CANADA 195

ANIMATION

'Animation is not the art of drawings that move but the art of movements that are drawn.' Norman McLaren, 1914–1987

Animation is an immersive experience; the optical illusion of movement is employed with persistence of vision.

Early optical devices and mechanical toys include the Thaumatrope (early 19th century), which was a twirling disc attached to two pieces of string. There was also the Phenakistoscope, which was a spinning wheel with cut viewing slits invented by Joseph Plateau in 1832. The Zoetrope, a revolving circular drum with slits inside the drum to view drawings animated on cards, was introduced by William Horner in 1834.

Emile Reynaud developed the Praxinoscope and opened the *Théatre Óptique* in Paris in the 1890s, the first movie theatre to show animated drawings. Another key figure in the development of sequential image-making was Eadweard Muybridge with his photographic series of animals and people in motion.

Animation dates back to the birth of cinema and comes in many forms, using many techniques including cut-out, stop-motion, silhouettes, models and puppets, pixilation, clay or clay-mation, 2D, 3D, digital, drawn directly on to film, painting on glass, pin screen and sand animation, and webtoons (online cartoons).

Many animated films make use of the technique of discontinuity to create humour. Paul Wells stated in *Understanding Animation*, 1998, *'when two ideas that do not seem to naturally relate, meet and indeed fundamentally conflict, this can create a comic effect. The joke comes out of a resistance to logical continuity.'*

The most influential and innovative animators include Tex Avery, Joseph Barbera, Walt Disney, Max Fleischer, Friz Freleng, John Halas, Joy Batchelor, Norman McLaren, Ub Iwerks, Oskar Fischinger, William Hanna, Chuck Jones, Winsor McCay, Lotte Reiniger, Osamu Tezuka, Len Lye, Ladislas Starevich, Terry Gilliam, Caroline Leaf, Frank Thomas, John Lasseter and Hayao Miyazaki.

Norman McLaren – Film Poster (left)

One sheet poster for *Neighbors* – a film by pioneering artist and animator Norman McLaren. © 1952 National Film Board of Canada.

SEQUENTIAL IMAGES: ANIMATION

Eclectic Trawl

'Fantasy, if it is really convincing, can't become dated for the simple reason that it represents a flight into a dimension that lies beyond the reach of time.' Walt Disney

An eclectic trawl through the following work will provide you with animation's finest moments:

Fantoche, the first animated character drawn by Émile Cohl (1908) (Fantasmagorie); Winsor McCay's *Gertie the Dinosaur* (1914) and *Sinking of the Lusitania* (1918); *Steamboat Willie*, the first film featuring Mickey Mouse by Walt Disney (1929); Otto Messmer's *Felix the Cat* (1919); Hayao Miyazaki's *Spirited Away* and *Howl's Moving Castle*; Caroline Leaf's paint-on-glass films *The Street* and *The Owl Who Married a Goose* (clay-mation); Matt Groening's *The Simpsons*; Tim Burton's *The Nightmare Before Christmas* directed by Henry Selick; Tim Burton's *Corpse Bride* (2005); Kihachiro Kawamoto's puppet animation *House of Flame*; the antics of *Tom and Jerry* (MGM); animated sequences for *Charge of the Light Brigade* (1968), *What's New Pussycat?* (1965), and *Who Framed Roger Rabbit?* (1988) by Richard Williams (live action, animation mix); *Lines Vertical* and the strong social message film *Neighbors* (1952) by Norman McLaren; Yury Norshtein cut-out style *Tale of Tales*; paper cut-out silhouettes of Lotte Reiniger's *Hansel and Gretel*; the abstract computer work of William Latham; the output of the Zagreb studios, for example, *Perpetuo* by Josko Marusic; the work of the Czech surrealist Jan Svankmajer, for example, *Alice* (1988), *Dimensions of Dialogue* (1982), *Faust* (1994), *Sileni* (2005); the cut-outs of Terry Gilliam for *Monty Python's Flying Circus*; the stop-motion models of Ray Harryhausen, such as *Jason and the Argonauts,* and Willis O'Brien, for example, *King Kong*; George Dunning's *Yellow Submarine* designed by Heinz Edelmann; *The Secret Adventures of Tom Thumb* by Dave Borthwick (Bolex Brothers); the stop-motion work of the Brothers Quay; William Kentridge's *Stereoscope* (1999); *Fantasia* by Walt Disney (principal animators Ward Kimball and James Algar); Paul Terry's studio Terrytoons and their series *Mighty Mouse*, *Deputy Dawg* and *Heckle and Jeckle*; John Lasseter's Pixar animations, for example, *Toy Story* and *A Bug's Life*; Nick Park's *Wallace and Gromit* and *Creature Comforts*; Sylvain Chomet's *Belleville Rendez-vous* (2003); and Richard Linklater's digitally filmed interpolated rotoscope movie *A Scanner Darkly*.

Description:
Image by prolific
artist and illustrator
Jon Burgerman

Animation on TV
From the 1950s, animated cartoons appeared on Saturday morning and early evening TV slots.

'In the lands of the North where the black rocks stand guard against the cold sea, in the dark night that is very long, the men of the Northlands sit by their great log fires and they tell a tale....' This was the introduction to each episode in Oliver Postgate and Peter Firmin's *Noggin the Nog* saga. Their company was called Small Films and created 12 books and five TV series of *Noggin the Nog* between 1961 and 1968. They are also responsible for *Pogles Wood*, *Clangers*, *Bagpuss*, *Ivor the Engine* and *Pingwings*.

Author and artist John Ryan also pioneered the use of limited caption animation using cardboard levers and pullaways and brass paperclips to animate his *Captain Pugwash* characters.

John Ryan's *Captain Pugwash* appeared in picture books and animated films broadcast on BBC TV between 1957 and 1966 and 1974 to 1975. His other series included *Sir Prancelot* and *Mary, Mungo and Midge*. Brian Cosgrove and Mark Hall set up Cosgrove Hall animation company in Manchester, England, producing the popular *Postman Pat*, *Chorlton and the Wheelies*, *Dangermouse* and *Count Duckula* for television.

'One banana, two banana, three banana, four. Four bananas make a bunch and so do many more. Over hill and highway, the banana buggies go, coming on to bring you the Banana Splits Show.' The colourful and strange Saturday morning TV show, *The Banana Splits and Friends Show* (1968–1970), produced by Hanna Barbera, featured the antics of Fleagle, Bingo, Drooper and Snork who would *'flip like a pancake and pop like a cork'*. The show introduced a number of animated series, including The *Arabian Nights*, *Three Musketeers* and *Danger Island*.

The spirit of the absurd and bizarre was also evident in H. R. Pufnstuf and the surreal work of the Brothers Grimm influenced *The Singing Ringing Tree*. Produced by the East German studio DEFA in 1957 and directed by Francesco Stefani, *The Singing Ringing Tree* (also known as *Das Singende Klingende Baumchen)* was broadcast on the BBC in the 1960s and 1970s, leaving its mark on a whole generation.

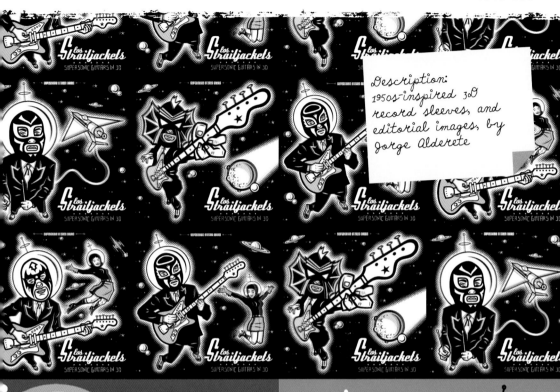

Description:
1950s-inspired 3D
record sleeves, and
editorial images, by
Jorge Alderete

SEQUENTIAL IMAGES: ANIMATION ON TV

Description:
Retro 'noggins' book
designed and printed
by artist/collector
Mark Pawson

NOGGINS+
WHAT ARE THEY?

Noggins are small handmade Viking ornaments – stylised figures of Vikings with wooden bodies and furry beards, they wear horned helmets and come armed with spears and shields. They're both war-like and cute – fluffy but ready for a fight.

They originated as tourist souvenirs from the Scandinavian countries – Norway, Sweden, Denmark, & Iceland and a thousand years after the original Vikings sailed on their epic journeys of conquest and exploration. Noggins set out from Scandinavia, invading people's homes and settling on knick-knack shelves and mantelpieces around the world!

Mark Pawson has spent 5 years collecting and researching Noggins, and amassing a private army of wooden Viking warriors – all pictured inside. With an artist's eye for detail and the passion of an obsessed collector, this unique book provides a fascinating look at the many different types of Noggins and some of their close relatives.

MARK PAWSON.
P.O. BOX 664.
LONDON E3 4QR U.K.
WWW.MPAWSON.DEMON.CO.UK
WWW.MPAWSON.DEMON.CO.UK/NOGGINS

CONTENTS:

INTRODUCTION:
NOGGINS? VIKINGS?
WHAT'S THEIR APPEAL?
DESIGN & MATERIALS
RESEARCH & DEVELOPMENT

WHAT ARE THEY?
WHERE DO THEY COME FROM?
WHAT ARE THEY FOR?
BACKGROUND & HISTORY
ANATOMY OF A NOGGIN

MEET THE NOGGINS:
BARE WOOD & A BIT OF CHARACTER
SMALL AND SPIKY
FUR OF MANY COLOURS
FOOD AND DRINK
CAVEMEN, BARBARIANS & SAVAGES
THE TARTAN ARMY
PLANET OF THE APES
OTHER MUTANTS & NATIONALITIES

CLASSIC NOGGINS
HIGH AND MIGHTY
MADE IN BRITAIN
FURBALLS
PLUG-IN VIKINGS
TRICK OR TREAT
ANOTHER DRINK?
GONKS GO BEAT

APPENDIX

BIBLIOGRAPHY

PRINTED ON RISOGRAPH GR 3770 AND
REX ROTARY 1290 COPYPRINTER AT
NIJMEEGSE UNIVERSELE
STENCILDRUK NETHERLANDS
OCTOBER 2001

SEQUENTIAL IMAGES : ANIMATION ON TV

Cult Cartoons

Cartoons are now available through cable, satellite, DVD and the Internet.

Back in the days of analogue television, kids would gather around the TV on Saturday mornings to watch the latest adventures of their favourite characters.

The following animated series appeared on UK television and have now gained cult status by the passage of time:

Watch with Mother, children's TV puppet shows, (for example, *The Woodentops*, *The Flowerpot Men*, *Pinky and Perky*, *Andy Pandy*), *Captain Pugwash* (1957–1966), *Huckleberry Hound* (1958–1962), *Gerald McBoing Boing* (1956–1958), *Yogi Bear* (1958–1988), *Felix the Cat* (1958–1960), *The Magic Roundabout* (1964–1971), *Marine Boy* (1968–1969), *Astro Boy* (1963–1964), *Top Cat* (1961–1962), *Wacky Races* (1969–1970), *The Flintstones* (1960–1966), *Rocket Robin Hood* (1966–1969), *Shazzan* (1967–1969), *Scooby Doo Where Are You?* (1969–1972 and continued later), *Jetsons* (1962–1963), *Adventures of Batman and Robin the Boy Wonder* (1969–1970), *Mary, Mungo and Midge* (1960), *The Addams Family* (1974), *Bagpuss* (1974), *Flash Gordon* (1979–1981), *Hong Kong Phooey* (1974–1975), *The Jackson Five* (1971–1973), *Wait Till Your Father Gets Home* (1972–1974), *Roobarb* (1974), *Danger Mouse* (1981–1992), *Dragon Ball* (1986–1989), *Dragon Ball Z* (1989–1996), *He-Man and the Masters of the Universe* (1983–1985), *The Transformers* (1984–1987), *Thundercats* (1985–1987), *The Simpsons* (1989), *Ren and Stimpy* (1991), *Beavis and Butt-head* (1993), *Mobile Suit Gundam Wing* (1995), *Pokémon* (1998–to the present), and *The Powerpuff Girls* (1998–2004).

SEQUENTIAL IMAGES : ANIMATION

Description:
Murderous cartoon
character based on the
notorious Victorian Jack
the Ripper by JAKe

Description:
Cult illustration work
by Stefan Marx of the
Lousy Livin' Company
in Hamburg

Video Games

Pong™ arrived in many children's homes in the UK on Christmas Day, 1975. Many hours were spent immersed in this simple table-tennis game.

Growing up in the 1960s and 1970s before computer games meant TV was in black and white and there were the tangible charms of drawing your own comics, stamp collecting, action men, model kit making, KerPlunk!, space hoppers and choppers. Once video games had arrived in the mid-1970s, they quickly evolved and grew into what is now a billion-dollar industry.

Games are now available in arcades, online and converging platforms, such as cell phones, MP3 players, PDAs, GPS receivers, digital cameras and watches.

Atari's Pong™ game had been a popular arcade game and the console version for TV spearheaded the computer game invasion. Constantly upgraded and evolving, these games have left masses of plastic consoles, leads, cartridges and CDs in landfill sites or have become collectors' items for nostalgic gamers. Hot titles included: *Asteroids*, *Tetris*, *Star Wars*, *PacMan*, *Mario*, *Pokemon*, *Myst*, *Lemmings*, *Sonic the Hedgehog*, *Megaman*, *Donkey Kong*, *Bomberman*, *Mortal Kombat*, *Doom*, *Final Fantasy*, *Sim City*, *Tomb Raider*, *Dragon Quest*, *Street Fighter*, and *Grand Theft Auto*. Atari released its 2600 video game console in 1977 and by 1985 had moved on to 16-bit consoles such as the Atari ST. Nintendo's hand-held game and watch Gameboy arrived in the late 1980s along with the Sega Mega Drive.

In the 1990s the Sega Saturn and Sony Playstation were introduced with their 32-bit technology. Nintendo pushed things to 64-bit with their Nintendo 64 console in 1996. Sony released its Playstation portable in 2005 and Microsoft entered the market with its Xbox.

The range of computer games is enormous and categories include arcade styled games, beat 'em ups, platformers, artgames, educational, shoot 'em ups, combat, quiz, word, survival, game controlled environments, vehicle based, flight simulators, player-controlled environments, third-person shooters, online role playing, puzzles, maze, city building, strategy, sports, board, card, real-time strategy games, tactical role playing, open source, historical settings and virtual pets. People now spend more and more time living in simulated reality, playing, networking and doing business. Millions have avatars, subscribing to online games and virtual worlds such as Second Life.

SEQUENTIAL IMAGES: ANIMATION

Description:
The author's first
video game console
from the mid-1970s, the
Interton Video 2400!

Description: (overleaf)
A retro game remake for
the Internet designed by
Austin at NEW for
Safetycat Inc. circa 1997

INTERTON VIDEO 2400

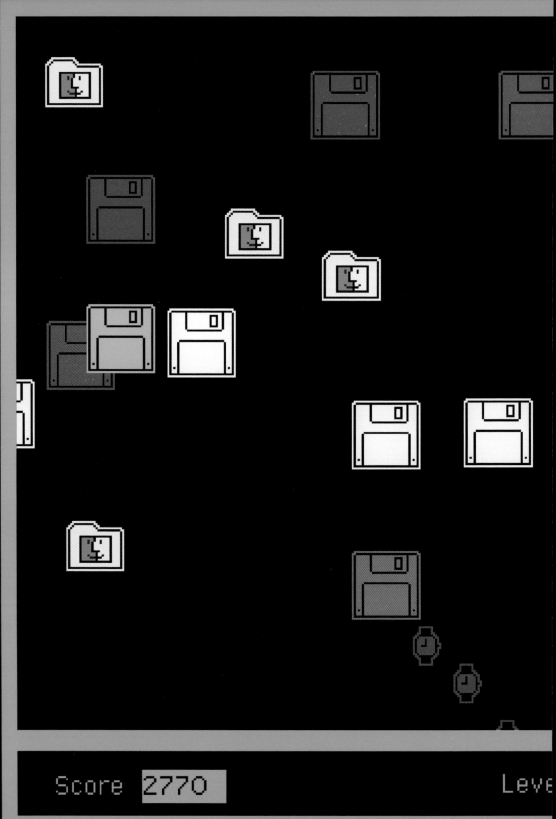

Score 2770   Leve

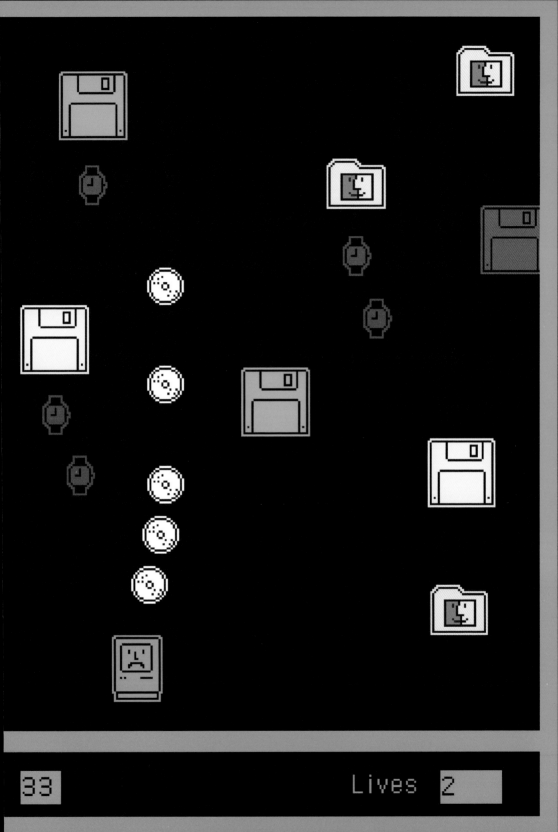

Lives 2

Description:
Black Convoy at the premiere of the 'BC3d' moving image experiment at the Hayward for Onedotzero 10

MOVING IMAGE

Motion graphics is a synthesis of the skill-sets of graphic designers, illustrators and animators. It integrates film, animation, graphics and sound. It spans music videos, short films, computer games, digital effects, installations, new media, film title sequences, TV commercials, animated stings, idents, 3D graphics and environmental design.

It is very much a product of the convergence of media available to the artist through the development of desktop digital film-making. This cross-media area blurs definitions and is constantly creating new hybrid forms and contexts. As in any artistic activity, there are pioneers who are taking the field forward and there are many pale imitators creating derivative commercial work following on their heels. Weak ideas can not be hidden by slick and seductive digital software effects. Concepts, idea generation, research, storyboarding, design skills and visual flair remain essential components in the creation of sequential moving image-making.

The antecedents of motion graphics were the early inventors of motion pictures and trick cinematography, for example, the Lumière Brothers, Milies and the experimental films of the avant-garde, Oskar Fischinger, Man Ray, Buñuel, Hans Richter, Vertov, Léger and animators such as Len Lye and Norman McLaren.

Motion graphics is a highly challenging experimental and imaginative field. Techniques used can range from the handcrafted to sophisticated digital pyrotechnics. Contemporary tools utilised to integrate time, space, motion and sound include the software program After-Effects, which has been described as Photoshop for moving images. Other tools for creating dynamic titles, 3D elements, special effects, character animation, organic camera paths, image processing and composites include New Tek Lightwave, Maxon Cinema 4D, 3D Studio Max, Maya, Motion, Final Cut Pro and Soft Image XS1, digital cameras, scanners and of course pencils and paper and the imagination to use them.

Designers, illustrators, animators and artists at the forefront of this field include Pleix, Johnny Hardstaff, Tim Hope, Shynola, Light Surgeons, Graphickers, Tomato, Attik, Geoff McFetridge, Tanaka Noriyuki, Furifuri, Geoffroy de Crecy, Psyop, Tanaka Hideyuki, Power Graphixx, UVA, Richard Kenworthy, Fuel, Intro, Mike Mills, Michel Gondry, Momoco, Olivier Kuntzel and Florence Deygas, Chris Cunningham and Spike Jonze.

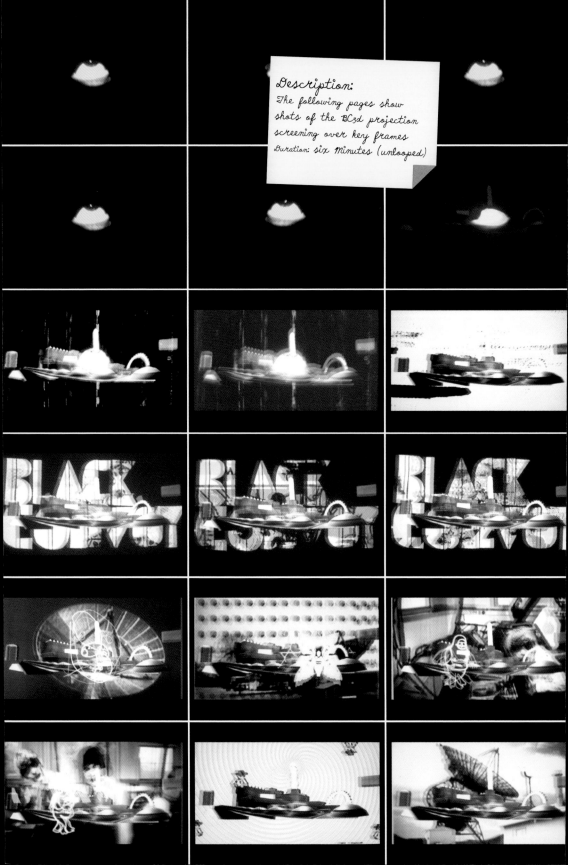

Description:
The following pages show
shots of the BC3d projection
screening over key frames
Duration: six minutes (unlooped)

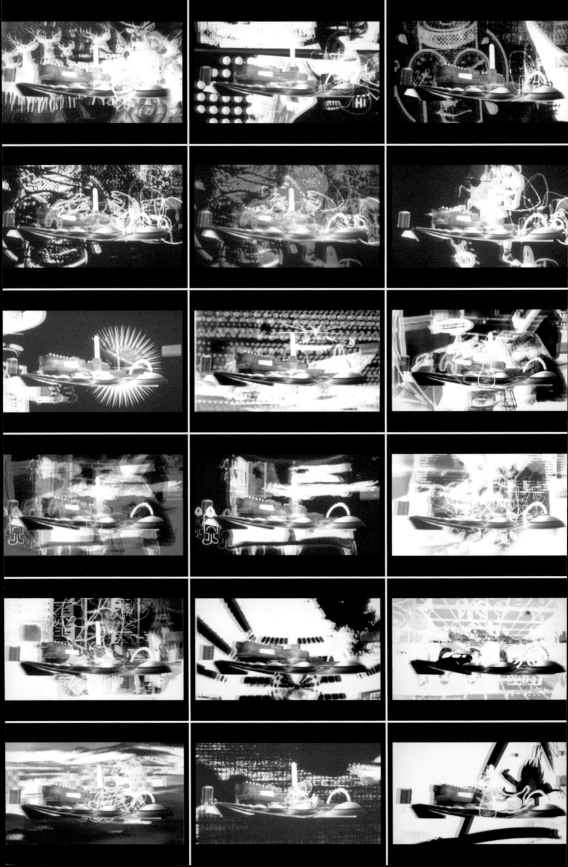

Title Sequences

'My initial thoughts about what a title can do was to set mood and the prime underlying core of the film's story, to express the story in some metaphorical way. I saw the title as a way of conditioning the audience, so that when the film actually began, viewers would already have an emotional resonance with it.' Saul Bass

Graphic designer Saul Bass was a leading pioneer in the development of motion graphics. His bold, powerful and simple posters and title sequence designs for films such as *The Man with the Golden Arm*, *North by Northwest*, *Vertigo*, *Psycho*, *Anatomy of a Murder*, *Cape Fear*, *Goodfellas* and *Casino* have proved to be highly influential.

Exemplars of film title sequence design include Maurice Binder, who designed 14 of the James Bond film titles, and Robert Brownjohn, who designed *Goldfinger* and *From Russia with Love*. Pablo Ferro, who started his career as a science fiction comic book artist, has designed numerous imaginative titles, including Stanley Kubrick's *Dr. Strangelove or How I Learned to Stop Worrying and Love the Bomb*, *A Clockwork Orange*, *LA Confidential*, *Thomas Crown Affair* and *Beetlejuice*.

Other ground breaking examples include Stephen Frankfurt's original titles for *To Kill a Mockingbird*, Olivier Kuntzel and Florence Deygas' retro title sequence for *Catch Me if You Can*, and Richard Greenberg Associates' (RGA) titles for *Alien*, *Superman the Movie*, *Altered States* and *Flash Gordon*. RGA's output has expanded into TV commercials, print, opticals and visual effects, as well as motion picture trailers. Kyle Cooper and Imaginary Forces have been at the forefront of motion graphics since the mid-1990s, their film credits including *Se7en*, *Spiderman*, *The Mummy*, *The Island of Dr Moreau* and *Dawn of the Dead*. Imaginary Forces is a multidisciplinary company based in New York and Hollywood; its activities have expanded into feature film production and marketing, corporate branding, advertising, network branding, marketing, architecture and experience design.

arts AND RAFtS
arts AND CRAFtS
NOGGIN
noggin.com
critter corner
Move to the Music
NOGGIN
noggin.com
STORy time
arts AND RAFtS
arts AND CRAFtS

Description:
Four 60-second idents
by Melinda Beck in the
USA for the 'noggin'
children's show

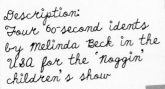

Experimental Film

Experimental film questions both the whole process of film-making and the audience experience of viewing film.

'The true method of knowledge is experiment.' William Blake

Time and narrative structures are often manipulated by employing rhythmic or in-camera editing and optical effects such as superimposition, time lapse, slow motion and pixilation.

The medium is associated with 16mm and super-8 film, multiple projection, loops, split screens, site-specific installation and camera-less film-making (painting and scratching directly on to film) and the use of optical printing techniques. The medium has exposed the world to some of the most poetic, disturbing, challenging and memorable sequential images ever created.

The experimental film tradition stems from the first use of the medium and from the early works of George Melies, such as the classic *A Trip to the Moon*. Apart from being a medium of expression in its own right, experimental film making has informed commercial music video clips, TV advertising, animation, the VJ culture, title design, motion graphics, video art and installation art.

Pioneers include: the Dadaists and surrealists such as Hans Richter, Jean Cocteau, Marcel Duchamp, Man Ray, Germaine Dulac, Viking Eggeling, Fernand Léger (*Ballet Mécanique*), Luis Buñuel and Salvador Dalí (*Un Chien Andalou*). The Soviet Cinema of the 1920s introduced the use of montage, fast film editing, which created 'linkages' or 'collisions' of scenes. Examples can be seen in Sergei Eisenstein's *Strike* (1925), *Battleship Potemkin* (1925) and *October* (1928) and in the works of Dziga Vertov and Vsevolod Pudovkin.

Poetic, oblique, impressionistic approaches continued in the works of Len Lye, Abel Gance, Jean Epstein and Lettrist film-makers, such as Isidore Isous and situationist Guy Debord, for example, *Howlings in Favour of Sade* (1952).

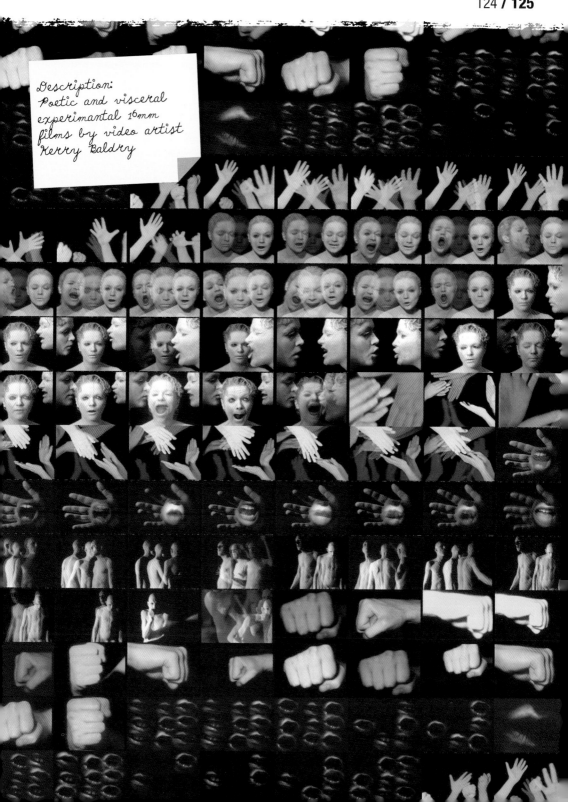

Description:
Poetic and visceral
experimental 16mm
films by video artist
Kerry Baldry

Description:
Work by illustrator Izzie
Klingels and animator John
Brown of the Soho-based
Popular Society

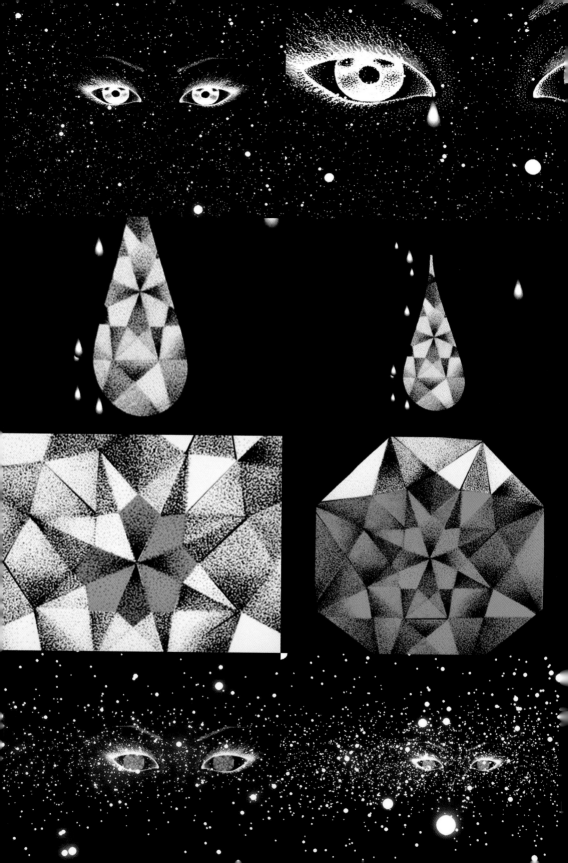

Counterculture

The 1960s and 1970s saw experimental film as a fundamental mode of expression for the underground counterculture. Influential works included 'Scorpio Rising' by Kenneth Anger, 'Dog Star Man' by Stan Brakhage and the films of Andy Warhol. The counterculture also fuelled the growing independent film movement in America and the new wave cinema of France, Germany and Czechoslovakia.

The era saw the development of what was termed structural film-making, which further deconstructed the film-making process and concentrated on flicker effects, single shots from fixed camera positions, time, frame, loop printing and form over content, as demonstrated in Fluxus films and the works of Yoko Ono, Michael Snow and Hollis Frampton.

In the UK, the London Film Makers Co-op (founded 1966) became the HQ for the British avant-garde film-makers. Film-makers such as Malcolm Le Gris, Mike Leggett, Marilyn Hatford, Annabel Nicolson, Jeff Keen and Guy Sherwin extended the medium into new territory. Further explorations in moving image and a blurring of boundaries occurred with the emergence of video art in the late 1960s and early 1970s (usually credited to the work of Nam June Paik).

Video art integrated elements of conceptual art, experimental film, performance and installation. Influential practitioners include Bill Viola, Bruce Nauman, Matthew Barney, Dan Graham, Douglas Gordan, William Wegman and Gillian Wearing. Video art has also merged with various artistic practices including architecture, design, sculpture and digital art. Some installations involve interactivity whereby the movements of the audience within an environment create a reaction.

SEQUENTIAL IMAGES: MOVING IMAGE

Description:
Kenneth Anger (left)
with independent UK film
maker, Nicky Abrahams
(right).

Photograph by Superduck

Description:
Miss Chievous, 2007
(variations on a theme)
by ApishAngel and PoW
artist nick Walker

Film Theory

There are numerous theories applied to film-making including Apparatus, Auteur, Marxist, Feminist, Formalist, Psychoanalytical, Structuralist, Genre, Ideological Formalism and Cognitive Theory. Here are a few definitions:

Apparatus
Apparatus theory draws on the writings of Jacques Lacan and suggests we see through the apparatus of mystification. The theory suggests that all cinema is ideological and reflects the dominant ideology of its cultural context.

Auteur
Auteur theory comes from the French word for author and implies that the film director is the fundamental author of the film. This theory was promoted by the director François Truffaut and is associated with the French new wave cinema (*Nouvelle Vague*) of the 1960s. Other directors who could be described as auteurs include Alfred Hitchcock, Jean Renoir, Howard Hawks and Fritz Lang.

Cognitive
Cognitive theory analyses ideas of narrative comprehension.

Feminist
Feminist film theory emerged as part of the feminist political movement and highlights the concept of the male gaze in cinema.

Marxist
Marxist theory can be seen in the films of the 1920s Soviet film-makers, for example, the importance of a group as opposed to individual stars in the Hollywood tradition. The Marxist influence can also be seen in the subversive use of parody, narrative and editing in the work of Jean-Luc Godard.

Psychoanalytical
Psychoanalytical film theory explores the narrative interpretation and poetics of classical Hollywood cinema.

Norman McLaren (pictured right) © 1949 National Film Board of Canada.

SEQUENTIAL IMAGES : MOVING IMAGE

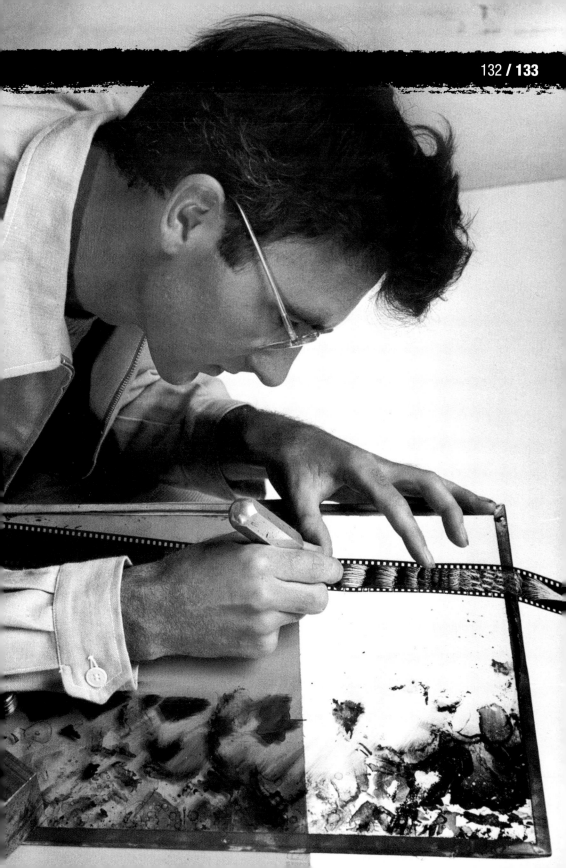

Genres

Films and books belong to specific categories; they also often cross, blur and mix the boundaries. An analysis of genres involves questions of narrativity, conventions and codes, subjectivity and authorship.

Literary genres and sub-genres that can be amplified and interpreted by the sequential image-maker include: children's literature, comedy, biography, autobiography, limericks, essays, fables, fairy tales, haiku, lyrics, adventure, whodunnit, crime fiction, detective stories, fantasy, mystery, horror, thrillers, conspiracy, spy fiction, political thinkers, science fiction, historical romance, family sagas, philosophical, satire, westerns and travelogues.

The main film genres are:

Disaster, fantasy, action, art, documentary, mocumentary, experimental, comedy, drama, family, new queer cinema, newsreel, film noir, neo-noir, tech-noir, horror, game show, Third World cinema, martial arts, sports, talk show, propaganda, science fiction, pornographic, spy, thriller, war, western, crime, biography, comedy, sword and sandal, mystery, silent, Wu Xia, historical, 3D film, sword and sorcery, musical, short film, animation, reality-TV, romance and screwball comedy.

Jamie Reid – Subverting genres

Upon graduating from Croydon Art College in 1970 Jamie Reid co-founded the Suburban press, which featured his agit-prop cut-'n'-paste graphics and situationist slogans. In 1976 he collaborated with Malcolm McLaren to work on his band the Sex Pistols. Jamie Reid produced the record sleeve for *God Save the Queen*, which featured an image of Elizabeth II with a safety pin through her nose, and the cover for *Never Mind the Bollocks*, which featured 'ransom note' typography. He also worked on the Sex Pistols' film *The Great Rock 'n' Roll Swindle* and has continued to collaborate with music industry artists designing music graphics, as well as painting murals and interiors.

Description:
'Peace is Tough' image
created by Jamie Reid
from issue 15 of The
Illustrated Ape magazine

Film Noir

'I hope they don't hang you, precious, by that sweet neck. Yes, angel, I'm gonna send you over. The chances are you'll get off with life. That means if you're a good girl, you'll be out in 20 years. I'll be waiting for you. If they hang you, I'll always remember you.'

Sam Spade in 'The Maltese Falcon' (1941)

Film noir or 'black films' is usually a term used to describe black-and-white films of the 1940s and 1950s, which dealt with themes such as crime, mystery, murder, detectives and gangsters. Early precursors of film noir were films such as *The Cabinet of Dr. Caligari* (1919), *M* (1931) and *Pepe Le Moko* (1937). These films were influenced by the German expressionist movement and incorporated what is termed *mise en scène*, meaning 'setting the scene', combining elements such as sets, actors, props, lighting and movement in a significant way.

The emotional tone of *The Cabinet of Dr. Caligari* is reflected in the design of the sets, which reflect the internal state of mind of the characters and story. Distinguishing features of film noir are low key and low angle lighting, the use of single source lighting, chiaroscuro, shadows, distorted, strangely angled shots and settings such as the city at night, nightclubs and warehouses. The city itself is often portrayed as a labyrinth of dark alleyways, wet sidewalks, seedy hotels and gambling dens populated by low life. Disorientation is often a key theme, with characters suffering from amnesia and paranoia. Narrative structures are often disrupted by flashbacks and flash forwards.

The dialogue of the characters contains witty slang and there is often voice-over narration. Archetypes featured include anti-heroes, femmes fatales, hardboiled detectives, corrupt police and down-and-out writers. The diagonal camera angles, juxtapositions and visual metaphors amplify narratives that feature moral ambiguity, obsessive behaviour, sadism and a sense of fear, menace and anxiety.

Description:
Image from 'never Ever'
by up-and-coming
illustrator/animators Echao
Jiang and Zoe Taylor

Post-noir

Noted directors of film noir include: Orson Welles, John Huston, Billy Wilder, Edgar Ulmer, Douglas Sirk, Fritz Lang, Otto Preminger and Howard Hawkes.

The genre has now expanded into post-noirs, neo-noirs, tech-noirs and cyberpunk tales of dystopic futures, for example, *Blade Runner* (1982), *Taxi Driver (1976), Raging Bull (1980), Basic Instinct* (1992), *Blood Simple* (1994), *Miller's Crossing* (1990), *Blue Velvet* (1986), *Mulholland Drive* (2001), *The Singing Detective* (1986), *Pulp Fiction* (1994), *Reservoir Dogs (1992)*, *Chinatown* (1974), and *L.A. Confidential* (1997).

In the 1940s and 1950s, film noir influenced comic book artists such as L.B. Cole and his work for Suspense Comics.

It continues to act as a source of inspiration for contemporary illustrators such as Geoff Grandfield who has produced illustrations for the box sets of Graham Greene and Raymond Chandler novels for the Folio Society.

The genre has also influenced many creators of graphic novels whose work has also gone on to be adapted for cinema, for example, *Road to Perdition*, written by Max Allan Collins (artwork by Richard Piers Rayner), *Sin City* by Frank Miller and *A History of Violence*, written by John Wagner (artwork by Vince Locke).

There is now a rich tradition of crime noir graphic novels, for example, *100 Bullets* by Brian Azzarello and Eduardo Risso, and *Chicanos* by Carlos Trillo and Eduardo Risso.

In the category of classic film noir the following are a must:

Citizen Kane (1941), *Sunset Boulevard* (1930), *The Third Man* (1949), *M* (1931), *Double Indemnity* (1944), *Touch of Evil* (1958), *The Big Sleep* (1946), *The Maltese Falcon* (1941), *Strangers on a Train* (1941), *Notorious* (1946), *The Naked City* (1948), *Fear in the Night* (1947), *Out of the Past* (1947), *Kiss Me Deadly* (1955), *Key Largo* (1948), *White Heat* (1949), *High Sierra* (1941), *The Lost Weekend* (1945) and *They Drive by Night* (1940).

Description:
A collaborative
illustration between
Neasden Control Centre
and Lee Ford

Description:
Image used on the flyered
invitation to a Crystal
Vision AV mash-up in the
summer of 2007

'We look for images, create them, manipulate them and mix them and finally put them altogether and try to tell a story.' VJ Tom Edom, VAIA
2005 International Video Art Show at Alcol Catalogue

Recent years have seen the growth of a new breed of sequential image-maker, the VJ or Video Jockey. Working alone or in crews, the VJ performs at events such as nightclubs, art events, concerts and festivals; just like the DJs they sample, scratch and cut to the rhythm of the music. They orchestrate video and film projected on large screens. The activity can be traced back to the screening of avant-garde Dadaist or surrealist films and the 1960s underground experimental 'happenings' and psychedelic light shows such as Andy Warhol's The Exploding Plastic Inevitable and London's UFO Club.

Intermedia artists such as Ronald Nameth and Aldo Tambellini created electro media environments integrating elements such as computer films, performances, audience participation, sound and multiple slide and film projection. Tambellini's *Black Zero* of 1965 featured hundreds of hand-painted films and slides projected as part of his Black Gate Electromedia Theatre in New York. At this time Carolee Schneemann initiated environmental or kinetic theatre, drawing inspiration from the 'happenings' of the time. Her projects involved projections, performances, audience participation and sound. Organisations such as Experiments in Art and Technology (EAT) were also pushing the envelope with real-time panoramic holographic and computer films. Large audiences encountered the spirit of invention in 3D movies, psychedelic sequences in major films, such as *Midnight Cowboy* and the Stargate corridor sequence in Stanley Kubrick's *2001: A Space Odyssey*.

This era of experimentation and exploration was informed by the writings of Marshall McLuhan, R. Buckminster Fuller and Gene Youngblood.

The Los Angeles collective Single Wing Turquoise Bird produced 360-degree light shows at rock concerts, such as the Shrine Exposition Hall in 1967 and 1968. Its maximal art employed overhead projections, liquids, slides, rheostats, multiple projection and the improvised use of a range of equipment. Its kinetic compositions were described as *'a combination of Jackson Pollock and 2001, of Hieronymus Bosch and Victor Vasarely, of Dalí and Buckminster Fuller. Time-lapse clouds run across magenta bull's-eyes. Horses charge in slow motion through solar fires. The hands of a clock run backward. The moon revolves around the earth in a galaxy of Op Art polka dots.'* Gene Youngblood,
Expanded Cinema, 1970

SEQUENTIAL IMAGES : AV MASH-UPS

Crystal Vision at the ICA

'Be engulfed by the endless wonder of a rare mystical creation mist…' this South London collective's AV mash-up involved film, video, fashion, sculpture, art, zines, comics, VJs, and DJs. *Holy Triangles*, *Big in Ghana*, *Joy & Pain*, *Pete & Jiro* and *Teens of Thailand*. Added to this

were musical interventions from two live bands, *Invasion* and *Of For.* All to create *'the general feeling that you are stuck in a Henry Darger painting with Shabba Ranx as your sidekick'*.

Crystal Vision, 2007. Images courtesy of Crystal Vision/Torie/ICA London.

Club Visuals

Club visuals became an integral part of the mid-1980s warehouse club scene in London with artists projecting their work looped on 16mm and super-8 projectors.

Industrial music bands such as Test Department and collectives like The Mutoid Waste Company and Psychic TV initiated multimedia spectacles in unconventional venues.

During the acid house days of the late 1980s, film technology and earlier 1960s technology, such as overhead projectors and oil wheels were joined by video projectors, strobes, dry ice and mirror balls. London clubs such as Shoom, Spectrum, The Brain, Love Ranch and Merry England experimented with themed visuals, unconventional screens, UV lighting, lasers and strobes, the mixing of slide projection, film loops, prisms and projectors. The Brain Club in London's Wardour Street drew its inspiration from Warhol's Factory and Cabaret Voltaire, and became the epicentre of the underground scene featuring seven nights a week of experimental happenings, such as The Sandal's Tongue Kung Fu, the live keyboard wizardry of Adamski and a Guy Called Gerald, the house music of the Hacienda's Graeme Park, brain machines, projections and psychoactive drinks.

At the large London Orbital raves in 1989, thousands of people danced all night to massive images provided by fractal generation programmes, sampled cartoons and video feedback edited to the music. The technology for VJs, both hardware and software, has continued to evolve, such as vision mixers using DVD players for scratching and real-time video playback.

Pioneers in the field include: Hyperdelic Video, who produced visuals for the underground techno scene in Tokyo in the early 1990s and in the UK, Vegetable Vision, The Light Surgeons, Coldcut, Hex and Hexstatic, Headspace, Scanner, D-Fuse, VJamm Allstars and Addictive TV.

Organisations such as Avit act as forums for the promotion of the work of VJs at festivals all over the world. Cinefeel and Addictive TV have been at the forefront of promoting hybrid fusions of aural and visual new media.

Festivals such as Optronica act as a showcase and include video screenings on plasma screens, interactive AV installations, multi-user audio instruments and new media performance.

SEQUENTIAL IMAGES: AV MASH-UPS

Description:
Addictive TV
specialists in music,
art, technology and
live VJing

Description:
stills from Addictive
TV's film remix
video 'Take
The Lead'

TAKE THE LEAD

ADDICTIVE TV REMIX

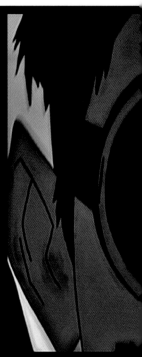

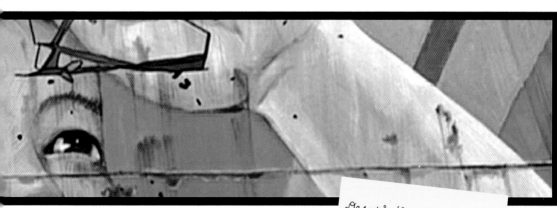

Description:
Stills from Addictive
TV's video
film remix
'Tekkon Kinkreet'

Description:
Addictive TV
performing live at
one of its hypnotic
audio-visual shows

Pick 'n' Mix Projects

For the student of graphic art, illustration prioritises process more than product. Different sequential media, forms and disciplines are radically juxtaposed, blurred and crossed, while also intensifying and amplifying the field of illustration.

In a nutshell, for the new generation of independent feral learners, double-click culture is almost transcending the role of tutors or even schools of art and design.

A new paradigm of illustration education is suggested, embedding the curricula with experimentation, fun, ethics, contradictions, play, debate and practical engagement.

Students are encouraged to select their own personal outcomes and programme of study.

SEQUENTIAL IMAGES: AV MASH-UPS

Description:
Performance headdress
by BA illustration
student Will Rigby

Pick 'n' Mix

Education and responsibility is emphasised over narrow vocational training and rigid academic conventions.

Real world focus and employability must go hand in hand with an unreal world focus and the development of the imagination.

Meaningful dialogue and participation is encouraged with learning outcomes generated by the learning itself and a move away from the grading experience of most art school assessment.

Images: Camberwell College, BA Illustration studios.

Sequential image-making projects have been provided on the following pages, consider a comprehensive approach to them. Orchestrate language and image, and if necessary time, motion and sound. Document your working process using logbooks or sketchbooks. Write, draw, research and generate visual concepts. Find your own way following your own voice, individual critical concerns and point of view. The development of your personal visual language should be underpinned by intellectual and practical engagement and an awareness of content and context. Confidence and visual intelligence is built through self-determination, motivation, ambition, passion, enthusiasm and a strong work ethic.

SEQUENTIAL IMAGES: AV MASH-UPS

DEVELOP a personal working methodology and strategies; articulate your methodology orally, through the written word and visually. Generate lots of ideas, know the theories, grow, achieve, synthesise material, be original and intellectually curious. Grasp principles, cross-fertilise, blur boundaries, take control, negotiate, evaluate, take responsibility, create new opportunities, think idiosyncratically, demonstrate reliance, autonomy and self-critical awareness, change the world, mean it, amaze, research, debate, multitask, fail, work, decide, organise, link, feel, adjust, monitor, astound, beguile, test, realise, redefine, resolve, communicate, think, draw, look, see, focus, articulate, visualise, target, manipulate, define, dance, critically debate, challenge constraints, collaborate, initiate, take risks, shout, work independently and ethically, play, deliver messages, explore, experiment, analyse, question, select, edit, interpret, employ media, laugh, evaluate, optimise, manage time, inspire, excite, enquire, innovate, simplify, subvert, entertain, sketch, doodle, brainstorm, mind map, storyboard, browse the Internet, wear a hat, visualise, report, tell a joke, manipulate and construct meaning, birdwatch, annotate learning log, observe, draw on the spot, employ visual memory, pogo, rewrite brief, adhere to deadlines, articulate a coherent personal direction and identity, close your eyes, educate, allude, evoke, convince, promise, think flexibly, agitate, identify problems and themes, wander, provoke, imagine, research, write, whisper, contextualise, develop concepts and personal strategies and values. Interpret text into image, relate image to text, control design elements and visual grammar and syntax of imagery. Challenge assumptions of visual communication and the present dominant production paradigm.

SELECT appropriate sequential media, for example, visual essay, animation, book, comic, video, installation, book art, performance, writing, sound, sculpture, dance, interactive media, film, architecture, ceramics, rug weaving, tapestry, flick-book, game, or photography.

MARKET your project: Destroy/create, do it yourself!

PRESENT and debate to peers, define agenda and direction within illustration, network, recognise strengths and weaknesses, demonstrate awareness of function, content, audience, copyright and client, as well as business, social, economic, professional, cultural, ideological, political and ecological contexts. Also demonstrate an awareness of critical debates and issues that directly impact on the field of illustration.

SEQUENTIAL IMAGES: PICK 'N' MIX PROJECTS

Project 1 – CARNIVAL

Produce a visual essay of six sequential illustrations based on the theme of CARNIVAL. Visual research includes Mexico's Day of the Dead and the illustrations of Posada, ancient Greek religious festivals, ancient Roman amphitheatres, circuses, clowns, jesters, fools, masques, Punch and Judy shows, the Burning Man festival, raves, the Rites of Spring, Mummers and Morris dancers, South American and Caribbean carnivals, Goya's Los Caprichos prints and *The Wicker Man* (1973).

Project 2 – MANIFESTO

'Art in its execution and direction is dependent on the time in which it lives and artists are creatures of their epoch. The highest art will be that which in its conscious content presents the thousandfold problems of the day.' Huelsenbeck from the first Dada manifesto, 1918

Illustrate a six-page manifesto of your very own utopian avant-garde movement. Research the manifestos, pamphlets and communiqués of the following: Futurism, Dada, surrealism, communism, Soviet LEF, Cobra, Lettrist Movement, Situationist International, Fluxus, Mail Art, Dutch Provos, Motherfuckers, King Mob, Yippies, White Panthers, SCUM manifesto and Class War.

Project 3 – INNER LANDSCAPES

Think and create sequentially, make a personal visual statement with seven interconnected images or scenes. This could be produced as film, video, animation, comic or visual essay. Consider paper engineering, for example, pop-up, folds etc. Initially write a synopsis outlining mood, tone, pace and key moments. Research and develop ideas. Experiment with materials. Create this series of illustrations based on the theme of inner landscapes. Research the work of John Cage, Samuel Beckett, Francis Bacon, Scott Walker, Howlin' Wolf, James Joyce, *Eraserhead* (1976) by David Lynch, *The Sleep of Reason Produces Monsters*, Los Caprichos series by Francisco de Goya, *Merry-Go-Round* (1916) by Mark Gertler, Edward Gorey, *The Wonderful Wizard of Oz* pop-up book by Robert Sabuda and *The Cremaster Cycle* by Matthew Barney.

Project 4 – ELUCIDATE THE TEXT

Produce a front cover and a series of six illustrations that highlight narrative tensions, conflicts, characters, beginning, middle and end, plot development and key moments from one of the following books: *1984* by George Orwell, *Lord of the Flies* by William Golding, *The Tempest* by William Shakespeare, *Metamorphosis* by Franz Kafka, *Slaughterhouse-Five* by Kurt Vonnegut. Research Walter Fisher's Narrative Paradigm theory, *Un Chien Andalou* by Buñuel and Dalí, and the animation of the Brothers Quay.

Project 5 – PUPPET SHOW

Design and build a puppet theatre, design puppets, video a performance or make a stop-motion animation that captures the mood, atmosphere and key dramatic moments of one of the following: *Psycho* by Alfred Hitchcock, *The Hobbit* by J. R. R. Tolkein, *Naked Lunch* by William S. Burroughs, *On the Road* by Jack Kerouac, *The Waste Land* and other poems by T. S. Eliot, *Dracula* by Bram Stoker, *Wuthering Heights* by Emily Brontë. Research Faust, Jan Svankmajer, *Spitting Image*, shadow puppets, marionettes and hand-to-rod puppets, wood and wire flexible armatures, and puppet animators, such as George Pal, Jiri Trinka, Henry Selick, Ladislas Starevitch, Hermina Tyrlova, Karel Zeman and Lotte Reiniger.

Project 6 – MINI-COMICS

Draw, design, print, distribute and sell or give away your own mini-comic. Keep the print run small and limit it to 16 pages. Decide on an appropriate format, size and shape for your comic. Make up a dummy, consider imposition of pages. The cover could feature use of colour, for example, silkscreen and different paper stock. Print the comic on a photocopier, collate, fold and bind the pages. Use a bone folder and a long neck stapler and a guillotine. Binding techniques can be as idiosyncratic as the rest of the comic – use of a sewing machine, Japanese 'pouch book' binding, hole punches, bolts or staplers. Research: Read lots of comics. Pace your story, develop a strong underlying idea or theme. Introduce variety and avoid monotony. Research *L'Association*, *Optimal*, *Ou-ba-po*, *Avant-Verlag*, Sins Entido and Small Press Expos.

Project 7 – DANCE STANCE

The dancer's movements reveal feelings. Through the use of illustration, capture the act of dancing as an expression of emotion, disciplined by rhythm and repetition. Create a visual essay of 12 pages of illustrations on the theme of dance. Research the underlying

SEQUENTIAL IMAGES :: PICK 'N' MIX PROJECTS

meanings of dances and their ritual significance. Select a dance form from the following (or create your own hybrid dance form): the belly dance, Sioux ghost dance, the dance of death, the waltz, the bunny hug, flamenco, tarantella, can-can, Charleston, Lambeth walk, capoeira, the sailor's hornpipe, Salome's dance, Dervish, lion dance, samba, and the devadasis.

Project 8 – PRE-VISUALISE

Create a storyboard for a film adaptation of a short story, for example, one of the Brothers Grimm's fairy tales from 1824 to 1826, Edgar Allan Poe's *Tales of the Grotesque and Arabesque*, 1839, or one of Geoffrey Chaucer's *Canterbury Tales*, *The Loneliness of the Long Distance Runner* by Alan Sillitoe, *The Mortal Immortal* by Mary Shelley, *The Legend of Sleepy Hollow* by Washington Irving, *Everything Goes* by Raymond Carver, or *The Book of Sand* by Jorge Luis Borges. Consider use of angles, point of view, eye level, continuity, dialogue and actions, framing of the shots, light and shade, key light, silhouettes, focus, atmosphere, foreground, middleground and background. Research *Le Jette* by Chris Marker, Alfred Hitchcock, Orson Welles, Frank Capra, Stanley Kubrick, John Ford, Jean Renoir, *The Secret*, *The Depository* and *Horace Dorlan* by Andrzej Klimowski, the work of Martin tom Dieck and Sergei Eisenstein.

Project 9 – INSTRUCT AND INFORM

Generate a sequence of illustrations that clearly provides information, for example, a recipe for a cookbook, travel guide, a chronological chart for a history book, a how-to book, an alphabet book or a children's encyclopaedia. Research: Bestiaries, emblem books, Victorian coloured toy books, gift books, hornbooks, battledores and chap books, also *Abstract Alphabet* illustrated by Paul Cox (2001), Kate Greenaway's *English Spelling Book* (1885), *The Galloping Guide to the ABC* or the *Child's Agreeable Introduction to a Knowledge of the Gentlemen of the Alphabet: P is a Peacock as fine as you please, Q is a Queen wears the crown with much ease* (ABC chap book published by Rusher of Banbury, 1810).

Project 10 – MIRROR, MIRROR ON THE WALL

Interpret a classic fairy tale, illustrate the book cover, content, endpapers; use vignettes and double-page spreads, and create narrative continuity. Change the historical context of the tale if you wish and bring it into the

21st century. Research: Mermaids, elves, trolls, witches, wizards, will o' the wisps, Beowulf, giants, Robin Hood, King Arthur, *The Singing Ringing Tree*, the films of Jan Svankmajer, *Pan's Labyrinth*, *Mirror Mask*, *Sleeping Beauty* illustrated by Gustave Doré (1862), *Fairyland* by the Brothers Grimm illustrated by Cruikshank (1824), and David Hockney's *Etchings of Grimm's Fairytales* (1969), Edmund Dulac, Arthur Rackham, Frank Frazetta, Marcel Dzama, Jockum Nordström, Alan Lee and Brian Froud, David McKean, Neil Gaiman and Hans Christian Anderson.

Project 11 – CAT PEOPLE

'The Owl and the Pussy-cat went to sea, In a beautiful pea-green boat, They took some honey, and plenty of money, Wrapped up in a five-pound note.' Edward Lear

Illustrate a story on the theme of cats. Research illustrators' representations, for example, Louis Wain, Wanda Gag and catcharacters such as Top Kat, Krazy Kat, Fritz the Cat, Pink Panther, Bagpuss, Tom and Jerry, Felix the Cat, Doraemon and Sylvester the Cat.

Project 12 – VERY SUPERSTITIOUS

Create a series of illustrations that interpret the theme of superstition, for example, magpies – one for sorrow, two for joy – a black cat crossing your path, seven years of bad luck from a broken mirror, walking under a ladder, opening an umbrella in your house, a rabbit's foot, horseshoes, touch wood and Friday the 13th.

Project 13 – STAND UP

Performances to be videoed:

a) Act out a charade, work in teams, choose titles and themes and interpret them using mime.
b) Write and perform a joke to an audience.

Project 14 – RIDDLE

Create a series of illustrations on the theme of a riddle; research puzzle books, rebuses, old English poetry, enigmas and conundrums.

SEQUENTIAL IMAGES: PICK 'N' MIX PROJECTS

The author has asked questions throughout this book. It is for the reader to seek associations and commonalities that can inform their own philosophy and practice.

Ask more questions, be critical, explore graphic art's social and cultural contexts and the underlying ideologies.

Cinematography

From *kinesis*, movement, and *grapho*, to record. Many illustrators and animators employ cinematic compositional effects in their work. A cinematographer constructs and composes a film by manipulating camera, movement, lens selection, exposure and lighting effects.

Eadweard Muybridge

(1830–1904) An English photographer who introduced the use of multiple cameras with timed shutters to record the motion of people and animals. He also invented the Zoopraxiscope to project his moving images.

FEKS (Factory of Eccentric Actor)

A 1920s Russian avant-garde collective that treated revolution as a carnival and found new ways to train actors while creating productions for both film and theatre. The group was founded in Petrograd in 1921 by Grigori

Kozintsev (1905–1972) and Leonid Trauberg (1902–1990). Their films assimilated genres and stereotypes from German expressionism, the gothic novel and the American western, while promoting Eccentrism.

Global Audio Visual Events

Organic collectives of artists and VJs directing and blending both sound and image. Contemporary pioneers include Addictive TV, D-FUSE and The Light Surgeons in the UK, VJ Culture (Grant Davis), USA, Dienststelle, Germany and Tokyo-based Ben Sheppee and Jon Schwark, lightrhythmvisuals. Recent global events include Visualux at Super Deluxe in Tokyo, Optronica, Futuresonic in the UK and Sonar in Barcelona.

Kibyoshi

Highly popular adult comic books produced during the late 18th-century Edo period in Japan.

A precursor of manga, Kibyoshi pictorial fiction featured social and political satire, narratives, humour and caricatures. The artist Kyoden made use of the term manga (whimsical or comic pictures) in his works of 1798. Although contemporary manga can be seen as stemming from this tradition, it has been heavily influenced by western comics and animation.

Limited animation

The use of limited movement, visual metaphors and abstraction. This technique saves money and time for animation studios. Fewer drawings are required than in films, which attempt to recreate realistic movement (for example, Walt Disney). Limited animation was used extensively by Hanna-Barbera and Filmation for cartoon series on TV. Examples include UPA studio's Oscar-winning *Gerald McBoing Boing* and *The Flintstones* series. The technique is also used in

Japanese anime and
Adobe Flash animation.

Marvel comics

Founded by Martin Goodman in
1939. Originally known as Timely
Publications and became Atlas
comics in the 1950s and then
Marvel in the early 1960s.
Comic book pioneers such as Stan
Lee, Jack Kirby and Steve Ditko
brought to life the world of Marvel
with characters such as The Mighty
Thor, the Fantastic Four, Spider-
Man, Captain America and the Hulk.
Many Marvel superheroes have
now been adapted into major
motion pictures.

Narrative

Derived from the Latin
narrativus 'telling a story'.
A narrative is basically a story, a
text produced in any medium that
describes a sequence of events.

Nouvelle manga

A comic art movement that focuses
on contemporary life and that
unites Franco-Belgium and
Japanese comic book artists. The
term itself was coined by
Comickers's editor Kiyoshi Kusumi.
Key artists of the genre include
Frédéric Boilet and Kan Takahama,
with books such as Mariko Parade
and Yukiko's Spinach, and Jiro
Taniguchi with the Walking Man and
the Times of Botchan.

Persistence of vision

This is a theory which has found
favour with film writers and scholars
and claims that the eye's retina
retains imagery for a moment,
thereby creating the illusion of
movement when viewing
a sequence of static images.

Rotoscoping

Frame-by-frame tracing of live-
action footage. The film is projected
on to a glass panel and then drawn
over. The technique was pioneered
by Max Fleischer in Out of the
Inkwell (1914). It featured in many of
Walt Disney's films, for example,
Snow White and the Seven Dwarfs
(1937). It was often incorporated
into TV animation, as in the work by
Filmation. Gradually the technique
has evolved with the introduction of
the computer digital FX, motion
tracking and interpolated
rotoscoping, such as Richard
Linklater's A Scanner Darkly (2006).

Studio Ghibli

A leading Japanese animation film
studio founded in 1985 by Hayao
Miyazaki, Isao Takahata and Toshio
Suzuki. The studio was built on the
success of Miyazaki's Nausicaa of
the Valley of the Wind and has
produced a number of outstanding
anime feature films by him, such as
Princess Mononoke (1997), Spirited
Away (2001), Howl's Moving Castle
(2004) and Gake no ue no Ponyo –
Ponyo on a Cliff (2008).

The Ashcan School

A term that was used to define
the work of realist painters
documenting the urban life of poor
districts of New York in the early
20th century. Robert Henri, Maurice
Pendergast and Arthur B. Davies
were part of a group of Ashcan
painters who called themselves.
The Eight. Edward Hopper has also
been described as part of
this group.

The Brandywine School

A school of art and illustration
established after 1900 by Howard
Pyle at Chadds Ford, Pennsylvania.
The work of Pyle and his students
such as N.C. Wyeth, Jessie Wilcox
Smith, Olive Rush and Frank
Schoonover became known as the
Brandywine School of Illustration
and their work featured in many
adventure stories, romantic books
and magazines.

The Folio Society

Established in 1947 by Charles Ede
and dedicated to the publication of
lavishly illustrated affordable
editions. The society has produced
fiction, histories, biographies,
humour, poetry, fairy tales and
classic children's fiction. Their
books are noted for their high
standards of design, illustration and
decorative book binding. Folio
Society books have been illustrated
by leading names in the field such
as Charles Keeping, Quentin Blake,
Francis Mosley, Paul Hogarth,
Paula Rego, Paul Cox and
many more.

Tunnel movies

With advertising space in short
supply on the Tokyo subway,
'tunnel movies' have been
introduced. A series of still images
are installed in the tunnel operating
like a flick-book. Sensors identify
train speed and illuminate frames
creating up to seven seconds of
LCD image.

CAVE ART

GREEK MANUSCRIPTS

GUTENBERG MOVEABLE TYPE 1440

CODEX ATLANTICUS LEONARDO DA VINCI

THOMAS BEWICK

GENERAL HISTORY OF QUADRUPEDS 1790

AZTEC CODEX

MEDIEVAL ILLUMINATION

THE APOCALYPSE ALBRECHT DÜRER

CHAPBOOKS

ALMANACS

ENCYCLOPÉDIE 1751–1772

GILLRAY

GOYA

TENNIEL

LA CARICATURE LE CHARIVARI 1830s

THE BOOK OF KELLS

PFISTER'S BOOK OF FABLES

THE DREAM OF POLYPHILUS

PHIZ

LEAR

GRANDVILLE UN AUTRE MONDE 1844

VELLUM

ANCIENT EGYPT PAPYRUS

JOSHUA ROLL(I0

DAS NARRENSCHIFF The SHIP of FOOLS SEBASTIAN BRANT 1494

WILLIAM HOGARTH 1697–1764

WILLIAM BLAKE

GOETHE & DELACROIX

RODOLPHE TÖPFFER

JACQUES CALLOT

GEORGE CRUIKSHANK

THOMAS ROWLANDSON

GUSTAVE DORÉ

KIRYŌSHI

ARTS & CRAFTS

PUNCH

LITHOGRAPHY
ALOIS SENEFELDER

OF NATURE
1844–46

HENRY FOX TALBOT

PHOTOGRAPHY

KELMSCOTT PRESS

DADA

EDWEARD MUYBRIDGE

LIVRE D'ARTISTE

WILLIAM MORRIS

SURREALISM

KATE GREENAWAY

AUBREY BEARDSLEY

PICASSO

MAYAKOVSKY

BONNARD

FUTURISM

SONIA DELAUNAY

MAX ERNST
LA FEMME
100 TÊTES

BEATRIX POTTER

HEARTFIELD

RANDOLPH CALDECOTT

ARTHUR RACKHAM

FB OPPER

WALTER CRANE

HOWARD PYLE

EMILE COHL

MATISSE
JAZZ
1947

R.F OUTCAULT
YELLOW KID

HERRIMAN
KRAZY KAT

OTTO MESSMER
FELIX THE CAT

HEINRICH HOFFMANN

WINSOR McCAY
LITTLE NEMO
IN SLUMBERLAND

WALT DISNEY

CHESTER GOULD
DICK TRACY

COCTEAU
MAN RAY

FRANK KING
GASOLINE ALLEY

HERGÉ
TIN TIN

WIGAN 07

VERTOV

EISENSTEIN

CARAN D'ACHE

LÉGER

ASHCAN SCHOOL NEW YORK

TREASURE ISLAND NC WYETH

TERRY AND THE PIRATES MILTON CANIFF

LEN LYE

BOB KANES BATMAN

HM BATEMAN

THE MASSES

DETECTIVE COMICS

PEANUTS CHARLES SCHULZ 1950

HEAVY METAL

TIJUANA BIBLES 1930s

MASSEREEL

TIMELY COMICS 1939

PLASTIC MAN JACK COLE 1941

STEVE DITKO

ART BRUT

THE SPIRIT WILL EISNER

POP ART

STAN LEE & JACK KIRBY FANTASTIC FOUR

MARVEL

SAUL STEINBERG THE PASSPORT 1954

HARVEY KURTZMAN MAD 1952

EC COMICS

JULES FEIFFER

THE BROONS

STAR

ROBERT CRUMB

WALLY WOOD

ASTERIX

LYND WARD

DONALD McGILL

RONALD SEARLE

REG SMYTHE ANDY CAPP

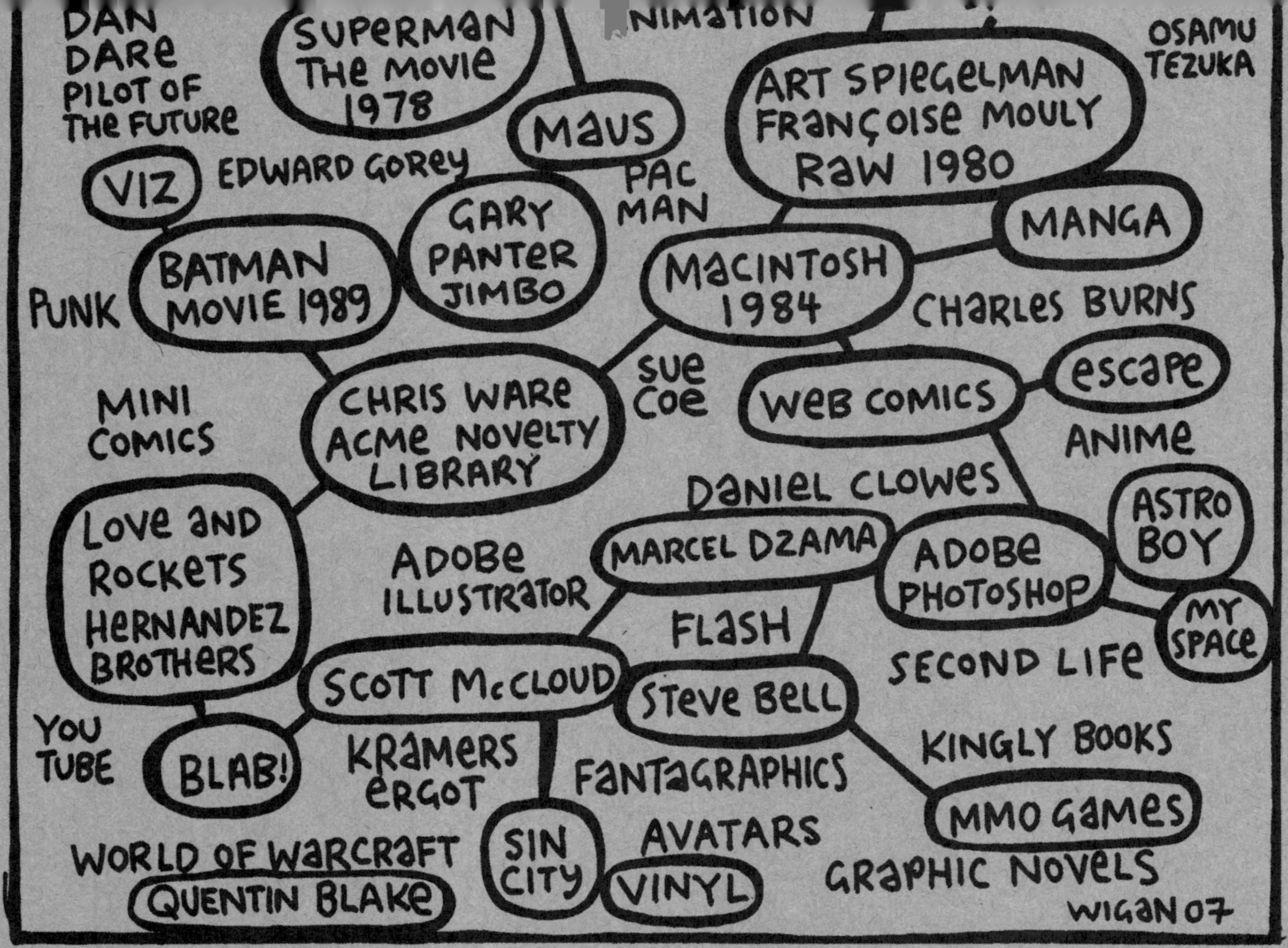
DAN DARE PILOT OF THE FUTURE
SUPERMAN THE MOVIE 1978
ANIMATION
OSAMU TEZUKA
ART SPIEGELMAN FRANÇOISE MOULY RAW 1980
MAUS
VIZ
EDWARD GOREY
PAC MAN
GARY PANTER JIMBO
MANGA
BATMAN MOVIE 1989
PUNK
MACINTOSH 1984
CHARLES BURNS
SUE COE
WEB COMICS
ESCAPE
MINI COMICS
CHRIS WARE ACME NOVELTY LIBRARY
ANIME
DANIEL CLOWES
ASTRO BOY
LOVE AND ROCKETS HERNANDEZ BROTHERS
ADOBE ILLUSTRATOR
MARCEL DZAMA
ADOBE PHOTOSHOP
MY SPACE
FLASH
SECOND LIFE
SCOTT McCLOUD
STEVE BELL
YOU TUBE
BLAB!
KRAMERS ERGOT
FANTAGRAPHICS
KINGLY BOOKS
MMO GAMES
WORLD OF WARCRAFT
SIN CITY
AVATARS
QUENTIN BLAKE
VINYL
GRAPHIC NOVELS
WIGAN 07

Reading List

Bell, R and Sinclair, M.
Pictures & Words:
New Comic Art and Narrative Illustration
Laurence King Publishing (2005)

Brunetti, I. (ed.)
An Anthology of Graphic Fiction,
Cartoons & True Stories
Yale University Press (2006)

Campbell, T.
A History of Webcomics
Antarctic Press (2006)

Carlin, J, Karasik, P and Walker, B. (eds.)
Masters of American Comics
Hammer Museum and Museum of Contemporary Art
Los Angeles (2005)

Crane, W.
The Claims of Decorative Art
Lawrence & Bullen (1892)

Dooley, M and Heller, S. (eds.)
Education of a Comics Artist:
Visual Narrative in Cartoons, Graphic Novels
and Beyond
Allworth Press (2005)

Dowd, D B and Hignite, T. (eds.)
Strips, Toons and Bluesies:
Essays in Comics and Culture
Princeton Architectural Press (2004)

Eisner, W.
Comics and Sequential Art
North Light Books (1994)

Gravett, P.
Graphic Novels: Everything you need to know
HarperCollins Design (2005)

Description:
A sample of comics and
periodicals
from the author's
own archives

Gravett, P.
Manga: Sixty Years Of Japanese Comics
HarperCollins Design (2004)

Hignite, T.
In the Studio: Visits with
Contemporary Cartoonists
Yale University Press (2006)

Jackson, H. (ed.)
The Complete Nonsense of Edward Lear
Faber and Faber (1947)

Kingman, E L.
The Illustrator's Notebook
The Horn Book Incorporated (1978)

Male, A.
Illustration: A Theoretical and
Contextual Perspective
AVA Publishing SA (2007)

McCloud, S.
Making Comics:
Storytelling Secrets of Comics,
Manga and Graphic Novels
HarperCollins (2006)

McCloud, S.
Understanding Comics
HarperCollins (1994)

Sabin, R.
Comics, Comix & Graphic Novels:
A History of Comic Art
Phaidon (1996)

Seth
Forty Cartoon Books of Interest:
A supplement to Comic Art No. 8
Buenaventura Press (2006)

Shulevitz, U.
Writing with Pictures
Watson-Guptill (1985)

SEQUENTIAL IMAGES : READING LIST AND USEFUL WEBSITES

Websites

www.WebComicsNation.com

www.BPIB.com

www.RunWrake.com

www.Comixpedia.com

www.SequentialTart.com

www.ComicsResearch.org

www.uComics.com

www.XericFoundation.com

www.Comic-con.org

www.TeachingComics.org

www.English.ufl.edu/comics/scholars

www.SocietyIllustrators.org

www.EgonLabs.com

www.TheSAA.com

www.TCJ.com

www.IJOCA.com

www.PixelSurgeon.com

www.DrawnAndQuarterly.com

www.IllustrationMundo.com

www.OneHugeEye.com

www.ThumbtackPress.com

www.AmateurIllustrator.com

www.TheiSpot.com

www.theLittleChimpSociety.com

www.BuenaventuraPress.com

www.CartoonStudies.org

www.ComiCartCollective.com

www.Typocrat.com

www.Fantagraphics.com

www.PressPop.com

www.Beguiling.com

www.theDrama.org

www.ThisIsRealArt.com

www.Lampoule.com

www.NewHatStories.com

www.WebComicsReview.com

www.PopImage.com

www.ComicBookResources.com

www.iComics.com

www.GraphicNovelReview.com

www.ArtBomb.net

www.ComicBookGalaxy.com

www.ComicsReporter.com

www.ComicsWorthReading.com

www.Pictoplasma.com

www.CartoonArt.org

www.TeachingComics.org

www.Cartoon.org

www.WordsAndPictures.org

www.OnlineComics.net

www.TheWebComicList.com

www.StashMedia.tv

www.DesignFlux.com

www.ICA.org.uk

www.BlackConvoy.com

www.JodyBarton.co.uk

www.RockwellClothing.com/Parra

www.LodownMagazine.com

www.Arkitip.com

www.ShawnWolfe.com

www.DazedDigital.com

www.OneDotZero.com

www.TheHorseHospital.com

www.BigActive.com

www.HelloGas.com

www.Shift.jp.org

www.Monsterism.net

www.homepage.Mac.com/james.jarvis

www.MediComToy.co.jp

www.KidRobot.com

www.StolenSpace.com

www.Faile.net

www.Mentary.com

www.WoosterCollective.com

www.Eatock.com

www.PicturesOnWalls.com

www.4wall.co.uk

www.ProductOfGod.net

www.BeautifulLosers.it

www.ModArt.com

www.IfYouCould.co.uk

www.GrafikMagazine.co.uk

www.CreativeReview.co.uk

www.Wikipedia.org

www.WordPress.org

www.OpenSource.org

www.Myspace.com

www.Bebo.com

www.FaceBook.com

www.Blogger.com/Start

Canon

Personal, meaningful and intelligent visual storytelling has a long history; it dates back to the first cave paintings.

Here is a canon of inspirational narrative image-makers, experts at interpreting and enhancing text and telling stories in whimsical, charming, beguiling and visceral ways:

Giotto,
Hieronymus Bosch,
Brueghel,
Grünewald,
Albrecht Dürer,
Rubens,
Eugène Delacroix,
Rembrandt,
Jacques Callot,
William Blake,
Hokusai,
Goya,
William Hogarth,
Paul Gavarni,
Thomas Rowlandson,
James Gillray,
George Cruickshank,
Phiz,
Grandville,
Honoré Daumier,
Sir John Tenniel,
Randolph Caldecott,
Walter Crane,
Edward Lear,
Kate Greenaway,
Beatrix Potter,
Louis Wain,
Toulouse-Lautrec,
Gustave Doré,
Edmund Dulac,
Arthur Rackham,
Howard Pyle,

N. C. Wyeth,
George Herriman,
R. F. Outcault,
Thomas Nast,
Käthe Kollwitz,
Diego Rivera,
Frans Masereel,
George Grosz,
H. M. Bateman,
Ernest Shepard,
Edward Bawden,
Edward Ardizzone,
A. B. Frost,
Norman Rockwell,
Mervyn Peake,
Al Hirschfeld,
Ben Shahn,
Saul Steinberg,
Harvey Kurtzman,
Paul Hogarth,
Charles Keeping,
Walt Disney,
Jack Kirby,
Osamu Tezuka,
Milton Glaser,
Walt Kelly,
Robert Weaver,
Hergé,
Jules Feiffer,
Robert Crumb,
Will Eisner,
Charles Schulz,
Marshall Arisman,
Brad Holland,
Tomi Ungerer,

Maurice Sendak,
Edward Gorey,
Art Spiegelman,
Sue Coe,
Eddie Campbell,
Dave McKean,
Frank Miller,
Steve Bell,
Peter Kuper,
Gary Panter,
Joe Sacco,
Dan Clowes,
Raymond Pettibon,
Seth,
Chris Ware,
Jaime and Gilbert Hernandez,
J. Otto Seibold,
Paula Rego,
Marcel Dzama,
David Shrigley,
Marjane Satrapi,
Quentin Blake,
Gary Baseman,
Paul Davis,
Henrik Drescher,
Sara Fanelli.

(This is by no means a complete canon, but a broad range of people well worth some further investigations.)

Cover image
Sequential Images cover 'Peoploids' image by Mark Wigan from *Wig Out*.

Conclusion

Writing this book has enabled me to feature artwork by leading edge artists and place this work in an historical and cultural context. I have drawn on some of the areas that have informed my own practice over the years including comics, animation, experimental film-making and multimedia events.

My earliest experiences of sequential image-making go back to the production of my own hand-drawn comics in the 1960s and 1970s. I would produce my own interpretation of Don Lawrence's *Trigan Empire* (Look and Learn) in the form of Dat and the Kadatans for my comic *Zoom*. The cinematic depictions of westerns, science fiction, football, pirates and war stories were a feature of action comics produced by D. C. Thomson and IPC (International Publishing Corporation). British comics such as *Victor*, *Hotspur*, *Lion*, *Tiger*, *Valiant*, *Hurricane*, *TV Tornado*, *War Picture Library* and *Commando Library* fuelled my interest in becoming a cartoonist.

In the early 1970s I became an avid collector of the output of American Marvel comics and the work of artists Jack Kirby, Neal Adams, Barry Smith and Steve Ditko and inspired by this, created my own range of superheroes.

A graphic design degree course at Hull College of Higher Education gave me the opportunity to continue drawing while creating experimental 16mm- and super-8 film. The cross-disciplinary nature of the course allowed me to create camera-less paint and scratch on film works, animation and multiple projections. After graduating in 1982, this multidisciplinary approach continued with record sleeve art work, nightclub murals, magazine illustration, self-published books of drawings, clothing ranges, animations for music videos and multimedia club events. This ethos of telling stories within a myriad of media and contexts remains relevant for the education of an illustrator.

For the student of contemporary illustration, the aim is to develop substantial originality in approaches to thinking, content and personal visual language. Confidence is key and is built through the development of fundamental skills in drawing from observation, visual memory and the imagination. Risk taking and experimentation should be encouraged with the use of a broad range of media from painting, drawing, collage and 3D to typography, photography, interactive media and moving image. Sustained idea generation and the use of sketchbooks is essential, as is intellectual curiosity and the capacity for broad and in-depth research. An analytical and critical approach to illustration is leading to the discovery of new media, territories and outlets for the discipline. Effective visual communication is enhanced through an authoritative knowledge of design principles and narrative structures. The student needs to demonstrate a well developed judgment in selecting, editing and synthesising sequential images. Working independently as visual journalists, entrepreneurs and authors, illustrators are publishing deeply personal stories with their own coherent and distinctive visual vocabularies.

'Art must unquestionably have a social value, that is, as a potential means of communication it must be addressed, and in comprehensible terms, to the understanding of mankind.' Rockwell Kent, 1882–1971

Basics Illustration: Sequential Images rejects traditional, defensive attitudes to illustration that simply allow the subject to constantly reference its past as its self-fulfilling raison d'être. This book asks the questions 'what is illustration?' and 'how do you educate illustrators to prepare for the future?'. Educators who advocate training and narrow vocationalism are perpetuating derivative and mediocre work and student passivity.

Diverse strategies, methodologies, theoretical frameworks and ideological positions must be questioned and assimilated. A deep approach to learning and learner autonomy is emphasised over narrow subjective dogma and uncritical training in software, craft and formal skills. The paradigm shift of emerging technologies presents new and unfolding challenges for the contemporary illustrator. Flexibility, creativity, curiosity and a breadth and depth of knowledge is required.

'Categorisation is a bullet to the brain. Learn how to side step beyond the firing line, or better still unload the guns. How could a humanistic approach deal with a communication process where speed, volume and scale rise above all other considerations? Coverage counts, not quality.'
Jon Wozencroft, *The Guardian Review*, 1998

The first rule of this new illustration is that there are no rules or boundaries, only opportunities. The second rule, if there was one, would be to take a position, make connections, speak out and publish your work. Illustration itself is a form of meaningful, cultural production and this book sets out to explode curriculums and dismantle pedagogies while embracing the cerebral, the contradictions, the irrational linkages, the meaningful and the sceptical. *Basics Illustration: Sequential Images* aims to inspire, inform and educate as it celebrates and documents the work of idiosyncratic international sequential artists and thinkers who are working in a wide range of contexts and media.

Acknowledgements

A big thank you to Kerry Baldry for help with researching and compiling information. Thanks to Austin Cowdall at NEW Studio for the brilliant design of the book. Also to the many contributors from all over the world who sent in images to support this book.

A thank you to Dave Woods and Phil Cosker, my inspirational film tutors on B.A. Hons Graphic Design at Hull College of Higher Education, 1979–1982. An acknowledgement to the colleagues and students I have worked with at Derby University, Coventry University, Central St. Martins College of Art and Design, Camberwell College of Arts and University of Salford.

Also a big thank you to Natalia Price-Cabrera, Brian Morris, Sanaz Nazemi and all at AVA Publishing for all their support, hard work and enthusiasm.

Images on pages 19, 20–21, 85, 86 and 93 courtesy of www.cartoonstock.com.

Images on pages 100 and 133 courtesy of the National Film Board of Canada.

Name	Contact	Page number
ADDICTIVE TV	<www.Addictive.com>	145–151
AIRSIDE	<www.Airside.co.uk>	23–29
Anthony Burrill	<www.AnthonyBurrill.com>	06
BLACK CONVOY (3D)		
Adrian Johnson	<www.AdrianJohnson.org.uk>	116, 118–121
Andy Potts	<www.Andy-Potts.com>	116, 118–121
Austin	<www.Myspace.com/AustinfromNEW>	116, 118–121
Gary Neill	<www.GaryNeill.com>	116, 118–121
Jon Burgerman	<www.JonBurgerman.com>	103, 116–121
Lee Ford	<www.LeeFord.org>	116, 118–121, 139
Mark Taplin	<www.TapLabs.com>	116, 118–121
McFaul	<www.McFaul.net>	116, 118–121
Neasden Control Centre	<www.NeasdenControlCentre.com>	116, 118–121, 139
Richard May	<www.Richard-May.com>	116, 118–121
Tim Marrs	<www.TimMarrs.co.uk>	116, 118–121
Chris Reynolds	<metropoppfield@yahoo.com	68
Clifford Harper	<www.Agraphia.co.uk>	75–76
CRYSTAL VISION		
Daniel David Freeman, Catherine Osterberg, Conan Roberts, James Tanner, Kristina Grundberg		
Lowadatone, Patrick Cole, Radical Animals, Rory Gleeson, Tome Merrel, Vox, Will Rigby and Xylol		
	<www.Myspace.com/WeAreCrystalVision>	140, 142–143, 153
FRANCIS ROVE		
Dennis Eriksson	<www.Stop-ill.com/Dennis>	12–15
Ed Gill	<www.EdGill.co.uk>	53, 55
Ed Pinset	<postmaster@soundprojector.demon.co.uk>	68
Frazer Hudson	<www.Frazer.dircon.co.uk>	51
Gomes aka Stefan Marx	<www.LivinCompany.de>	110–111
GREYWORLD		
Andrew Shoben	<www.Greyworld.org>	30–35
Horse Bites	<www.HorsebiteDesign.com>	65
IF YOU COULD		
Alex Bec & Will Hudson	<www.IfYouCould.co.uk>	17
JAKE STAR WARS		
JAKe	<www.JAKe-Art.com>	95–97, 109
Jorge Alderete	<www.JorgeAlderete.com>	105

JONNY-FU

Ron Jonzo	\<www.RonJonzo.com\>	98–99
Kerry Baldry	\<KerryBaldry1@yahoo.com\>	125

LE DERNIER CRI

Dr Marco	\<www.LeDernierCri.org\>	69
Mark Pawson	\<www.MPawson.demon.co.uk\>	106–107
Melinda Beck	\<www.MelindaBeck.com\>	123

NEVER EVER

Zoe Taylor & **Echao Jiang**	\<Zlysbeth@hotmail.com\>	137
NEW	\<www.NEW-online.co.uk\>	114–115
Nick Walker	\<www.apishangel.co.uk\>	130–131

PEEPSHOW COLLECTIVE

Andrew Rae	\<www.AndrewRae.org.uk\>	37–39
Spencer Wilson	\<www.SpencerWilson.co.uk\>	37–39
Luke Best	\<www.LukeBest.com\>	37–39
Jenny Bowers	\<www.JennyBowers.co.uk\>	37–39
Miles Donovan	\<www.MilesDonovan.co.uk\>	37–39
Chrissie MacDonald	\<www.ChrissieMacDonald.co.uk\>	37–39
Pete Mellor	\<www.Peepshow.org.uk\>	37–39
Marie O'Connor	\<www.SHOWstudio.com/contributors\>	37–39
Elliot Thoburn	\<www.ElliotThoburn.co.uk\>	37–39
Lucy Vigrass	\<www.LucyVigrass.co.uk\>	37–39
Rachel Ortas	\<www.RachelOrtas.co.uk\>	78, 81
Rosie Short	\<RosieShort@hotmail.com\>	94
Run Wrake	\<www.RunWrake.com\>	41–49
SAFETYCAT INC	\<www.Safetycat.co.uk\>	114–115
Scott Garrett	\<www.GarrettWorld.co.uk\>	61
Simone Lia	\<www.SimoneLia.com\>	82–83
THE ILLUSTRATED APE	\<www.TheIllustratedApe.com\>	135

THE POPULAR SOCIETY

Izzie Klingels	\<mail@IzzieKlingels.co.uk\>	126–127
John Brown	\<www.ThePopularSociety.co.uk\>	126–127
Wigan	\<MarkWigan@hotmail.com\>	56, 58–59, 162–165, 171
Yuko Kondo	\<www.YukoKondo.com\>	73
Zeel	\<www.Zeel.co.uk\>	66–67